THE S

Sidin Vadukut is one of India's most popular journalists, authors, columnists and bloggers. He is currently an editor with *Mint*, and is the author of the best-selling Dork series. *The Sceptical Patriot* is his first book of non-fiction.

Sidin lives in London with his wife and daughter. He tweets as @sidin and blogs at http://www.whatay.com.

THE SCEPTICAL PATRIOT

Exploring the Truths Behind the Zero and Other Indian Glories

SIDIN VADUKUT

RUPA

Published by
Rupa Publications India Pvt. Ltd 2014
7/16, Ansari Road, Daryaganj
New Delhi 110002

Sales centres:
Allahabad Bengaluru Chennai
Hyderabad Jaipur Kathmandu
Kolkata Mumbai

ISBN: 978-81-291-2903-1

First impression 2014

10 9 8 7 6 5 4 3 2 1

The moral right of the author has been asserted.

Typeset by Jojy Philip, New Delhi.

Printed at Thomson Press India Ltd, Faridabad

To
K and S

Contents

Introduction
Extensive Disclaimers

Hello. A new book! How exciting!

First of all, thank you for buying a collection of somewhat personal explorations into Indian history, by an author who has previously only written humour novels set in fictional management consulting firms. You have done a very brave thing indeed. And I am deeply grateful. I hope this book will fully reward you for your audacity.

Before you plunge into these explorations, there are two things about this book that you should know at the outset. Knowing these things may help you enjoy this book more.

First, almost everything you read in this book will eventually be proven wrong. This is the nature of most history writing, even when the writer attempts nothing more ambitious than trying to answer the question: What do you think really happened? History, in quotes, usually gets even more controversial when writers try to figure out not only what happened, but also the reasons for and implications of these happenings.

Much scholarship and punditry later, just when it looks like we have unshakeable proof to buttress some historical argument, new discoveries will come along and make everything before them meaningless. History is an enigmatic mistress who likes to keep her lovers on their toes.

As I sit on my sofa typing out these words, bookstores all around the world are being lashed by tidal waves of books on the First World War. There are now only a few months left for the centenary of that most terrible of human conflicts. And yet book after new book and documentary after new documentary still strives to answer that fundamental question: Why did the First World War happen?

A hundred years later—years that have been spent in relentless historical research, analysis and scholarship—there is still exuberant debate about why the Great War broke out. Who or what was responsible? British vacillation? German ambition? Russian mischief? Serbian intrigue? Austrian pomposity? Industry? Human stupidity?

If the First World War seems beyond historical consensus, what chance is there for this book, or any book, to make incontrovertible statements about millennia of brain-meltingly complex Indian history?

In my explorations for this book I have sought to tread lightly around and through controversy. The idea of this book is, admittedly, to question certain popular notions and narratives of Indian history. But I have tried to do so within the confines of established historical research. The idea is to take you on a series of short journeys into certain alleyways of Indian history without asking you to take sides on anything.

You are free to, of course.

On infrequent occasions in this book I have planted my flag on certain sides of some historical arguments. You are welcome, nay encouraged, to disagree with me on these conclusions.

But I implore to always keep in mind that the journey is paramount. Think of this book as one of those guided walking tours that tourists go on. If you wish you can constantly stop the nice man who is showing you around with your incessant questions and arguments, thereby ruining the tour for him, you and everybody else. Or you can take it all in, make a mental note of disagreements, and then revisit things later when your tour is complete.

The latter approach may help you enjoy this book better.

In any case, eventually, all our conclusions and analyses will be proven wrong anyway.

Just days before we locked in the final draft of this book, there were reports of a major new archaeological excavation in Nepal. A team of forty archaeologists led by Professor Robin Coningham of Durham University excavated a new shrine beneath the Maya Devi temple in Lumbini that potentially moves the Buddha's birthdate back by three-hundred years to the sixth century BCE.[1]

As you might imagine, this has a significant impact on a lot of historical research. Especially when it comes to events, people, or documents that hitherto had been dated with respect to the life of Buddha. Your author also had to make urgent adjustments to one chapter to reflect this discovery.

What is to say that many thousands of such discoveries lay buried beneath our temples, monuments, homes, forests, farms and even highways? Who is to say that within weeks of this book's launch a new excavation in Delhi or Sanchi or Tanjavur will render many of these chapters worthless?

This does freak me out a little bit. But that is history for you. Onwards she marches, making fools of us and our petty squabbles.

So that is the first thing you need to keep in mind—this book does not aspire to be the final word on Indian history.

[1]Elizabeth Day, 'Archaeologists' Discovery Puts Buddha's Birth 300 Years Earlier', *The Guardian,* 30 November 2013.

The second thing you must keep in mind before reading further is that this book was almost entirely typed perched precariously on the shoulders of giants. This book is the fruit of months of poking and prodding through books and manuscripts at libraries and numerous online archives. However this effort pales in comparison to the people who work at the coalface of history—digging up things, translating manuscripts, dating events, preserving objects and piecing together historical narratives one palm leaf page at a time. It owes everything to the work of at least two centuries' worth of Indologists and historians.

The chapter on the Chola expeditions, for instance, would have been impossible if not for the work of Augustus Frederic Rudolf Hoernlé, Georges Coedes and hordes of other epigraphists, researchers and scholars.

The debt of gratitude to them is huge.

But along with that debt comes a certain historical narrative thread. Pioneers in any field tend to set the terms of engagement between the public and their innovations and discoveries. So while we continue to analyze and criticize the works of Darwin, Newton, Keynes or Hayek, we are still bound in some ways to the tone and syntax of these pioneers and their work. (Or to what we think is their tone and syntax.)

This is perhaps why some Keynesians still think that Hayekians live in free market utopia, while Hayekians deplore the swagger and condescension of their posh Keynesian colleagues.

Students of history are equally prone to the same bonds of tone and syntax. Amateur students even more so. So do keep in mind that my efforts in this book have primarily been those of constructing an entertaining but accurate narrative of history based on the work of others. However it is inevitable that their biases and postures will have filtered through as well.

Indian history is particularly prone to this kind of thing.

Many of the most frequently quoted works and analyses of Indian history and Indology were written by people of non-Indian origin. Also, most of these books were written well before the establishment of the free Indian republic. If you go through the footnotes in this book, you will realize that most of my sources pre-date Indian independence. The majority also hail from foreign lands and foreign minds, so to speak. British and German names abound.

Also, I've limited my research to sources in the English language, or English translations of original texts. This automatically takes me at least one degree of separation away from many original source materials. Things can be lost in the translation.

Not that this automatically makes these sources biased or unreliable or in some way anti-Indian. Whatever be their political views, most Indologists of yore seem to have had a tremendous fondness for India and Indian history. But many Indians increasingly seem wary of foreign scholarship, and I think it is important to point this out here before you go in any further.

This book, therefore, is a pursuit for relative truths and not absolute ones. It has been written in good faith and is intended to be good fun.

Having said that, this is a work that celebrates scepticism and inquiry. Therefore, it should also be subject to the same values. Feel free to question my approaches and conclusions. Wherever possible, I have mentioned all my sources in footnotes.

Now that we've got that bit out of chitchat out of the way, let me tell you why I wrote this book and what it aims to achieve. It starts with a certain Justice Markandey Katju.

✳❦✳

In early December 2012, Justice Markandey Katju, a retired judge of the Supreme Court of India, was invited to speak at a seminar in New Delhi.

Like any other country in the world with a large and sophisticated judiciary, India too demands much of its legal minds before they are invited to take office at the Supreme Court in New Delhi. Justice Katju had been a lawyer and then a judge for thirty-six years before he was elevated to the Supreme Court in April 2006. It was, by most metrics and public opinion, a stellar career.

India has an uncommonly inefficient legal system. Courts in this country currently preside over some fourteen million pending cases, many of which date back over three decades. Public trust in the legal process is poor. For most Indians, courts are bottomless pits of misery where you only go when you want to make sure that your lawsuit never achieves closure. They are useful if you want to quash a business competitor, steal land from a brother or cousin, or simply harass a journalist for defamation.

Especially if you want to harass a journalist for defamation.

However, this distrust mysteriously evaporates at the gates of the Supreme Court building in New Delhi. In the minds of many citizens, the Supreme Court thrives in a dimension or even universe apart from the rest of the legal system. Somehow, the apex court is believed to be immune to all the corruption that pervades lower courts and magistrates.

Thus there is no more respected institution in the country than the Supreme Court, and no more respected office in the country than that of a judge of the Supreme Court of India. So much so that there is an element of intellectual celebrity in Supreme Court judges. Once they've retired from service, and are no longer bound by codes of court decorum, many are expected to speak their minds—and become lonely islands of virtue in a sea of corruption.

Justice Katju took to his retirement with uncommon gusto. He spoke the pants off his mind. It was as if he was making up for four decades of restraint. Within weeks of retiring from the Supreme Court, and after being appointed Chairman of the Press Council of India, he said this about Indian journalists in a televised interview:

> The majority, I'm sorry to say, are of a very poor intellectual level, media people, I doubt whether they have any idea of economic theory or political science, philosophy, literature, I have grave doubts whether they are well read in all this, which they should be.

The comments were met with nationwide delight and jubilation. In the mind of the Indian public, journalists currently occupy a position of respect somewhere between pond scum and Ebola virus. Katju had delivered a pitch-perfect aria.

Justice Katju could have stopped there. But Justice Katju did not stop there. He kept going. At a seminar in Delhi in 2012[2], he went one step too far. He delivered this full-bodied rant that has since passed into legend:

> I say 90 per cent of Indians are idiots. You people don't have brains in your heads... It is so easy to take you for a ride. You mad people will start fighting amongst yourself, not realizing that some agent provocateur is behind a mischievous gesture of disrespect to a place of worship. Today 80 per cent Hindus are communal and 80 per cent Muslims are communal. This is the harsh truth, bitter truth that I am telling you. In 150 years, you have gone backwards instead of moving forward because the English kept injecting poison. The policy that emanated from London after the mutiny in 1857 [said] that

[2]Seminar by the South Asia Media Commission, 8 December 2013.

there is only one way to control this country: that is to make Hindus and Muslims fight each other... Our ancestors also studied Urdu, but it is so easy to fool you. You are idiots, so how difficult is it to make an idiot of you?[3]

Calling journalists idiots was one thing. Calling nine out of ten Indians idiots? The outrage was instantaneous.

It wasn't that many people disagreed with the substance of Katju's pithy analysis. I think it is fair to assume that there are a large number of idiots in any given random collection of citizens of any country. The exact proportion of idiots is subjective. For instance, in some cultures, anyone who listens to Pink Floyd and was not born in the 1960s may be considered an idiot. Entire Indian engineering colleges would be idiots in this case.

The problem, I suppose, was not with what Justice Katju said but the fact that *he* said it. A retired Supreme Court judge. A man of broad and deep scholarship. A man who should know better than to resort to made-up statistics and punditry. What were journalists for, then?

Before Justice Katju even had a chance to 'clarify' his comments—another art form he has subsequently acquired mastery in—two young Indians served him a legal notice. Law student Tanaya Thakur and her brother Aditya Thakur said that they would sue the Justice if he didn't apologize for his statements.

According to one online profile[4], the Thakur siblings are

[3]'Media Deliberately Dividing People: PCI Chief', *IBNlive.com*, 30 October 2011.

[4]'Tanaya Thakur: A Teenage Girl of 17 Years but Walks on the Legendary Path', *Ground Report India*, 23 November 2012, from <http://www.groundreportindia.com/2012/11/tanaya-thakur-teenage-girl-of-17-years.html>, accessed on 3 February 2014.

serial legal notice servers. 'Tanaya,' it says, 'can turn ferocious when she finds that injustice is being done. Her life seems to be a struggle in the present for a better future.'

Shudder.

On 10 December 2012, Justice Katju wrote a post on his blog titled 'Reply to Young Students Tanaya and Aditya'.

The post almost sounds contrite. 'The figure 90% is not a mathematical figure,' he writes, 'it simply means that in my opinion a large proportion of Indian (and again I repeat, not all) are fools.'

The very next line, though, he parries: 'I never named you, nor any community, caste, or sect, and I never said that you are in the category of 90%. Hence I do not see how you are defamed.'

Katju goes onto explain his statements and his original intentions. And then, somewhat inexplicably, segues into a discussion on India's past greatness. I reproduce extracts from that portion here:

> But there was a time when we were leading the whole world in science and technology, and India was perhaps the most prosperous country in the world. It is now that we are having bad times, but we had a glorious past and shall have a glorious future too, but for that we have to get rid of casteism, communalism, superstitions and other backward traits in the mentality of a large part of our people (because of which I call them fools).

> **India's Past**
> With the aid of science we had built mighty civilizations thousands of years ago when most people in Europe (except in Greece and Rome) were living in forests… The way out of the present morass is to go back again to the path shown

by our scientific ancestors, the path of Aryabhatta and Brahmagupta, Sushruta and Charak, Panini and Patanjali, Ramanujan and Raman...

The decimal system in mathematics was the most remarkable and revolutionary invention in the past, and it was created by Indians. To understand its significance, one must know that the ancient Romans...felt very uncomfortable with numbers above 1000. This was because they expressed their numbers in alphabets, I standing for 1, V for 5, X for 10, L for 50, C for 100, D for 500, and M for 1000. There was no single alphabet expressing a number above 1000. Hence to write 2000 an ancient Roman had to write MM, to write 3000 he had to write MMM, and to write 1 million he had to write M one thousand times, which would drive him crazy.

On the other hand, our ancestors discovered the number 0, and hence to write 1 million they had simply to put 6 zeros after 1...

Plastic surgery was invented by Sushrut 2000 years ago, whereas Europeans invented it only about 100 or 200 years back...

Before the coming of the British India was a prosperous country. Its share in world trade in 1700 was about 30%, which fell to 2% by the end of British rule and is still not more than 3%.

The post goes on for a grand total of 1,841 words.

Shortly after posting, the comments began to flood in. That evening, a commenter calling himself venky-kadam posted:

Dear Katju sir,
I hope the justification will work for students to understand the facts, I appriciate [sic] the way of explaining through History.

But are these facts? Is all this history? Was the Justice stating historical fact? Or repeating popular myths? Surely someone who was a judge of the Supreme Court would know his fact from fiction?

Surely people in high places, equipped with education and scholarship, are immune to historical misrepresentation?

Perhaps somebody should check up on some of these facts about India…

⸙

On 10 March 2008, two members of the Rajya Sabha, India's Upper House of Parliament, exchanged a few cordial words in the course of a debate on education[5]. Dr Karan Singh is a veteran Congress politician and Daggubati Purandeswari was the then Minister of State for Human Resource Development. This is the record of their exchange according to the archives of the Rajya Sabha:

> **Dr Karan Singh**: Sir, before I put my supplementary, I would just make a submission that this is such an important matter that, if possible, in the second half of this Session, you could give us one day when the House could really discuss education in its depth. I am sure the hon. Members from all over the House, will be keen for it.
>
> My specific supplementary is this. Despite all weaknesses of our system, of our products, our IIMs, our IITs, and our medical colleges, have done very well around the world. Nonetheless, the Knowledge Commission has made certain important recommendations. Have those recommendations been brought before the House? Will they be discussed in

[5]Rajya Sabha Archives, from <http://164.100.47.5/newdebate/213/10 032008/11.00amTo12.00Noon.pdf>, accessed on 3 February 2014.

the House? Or, will the Government come out with a policy statement as to what exactly they are going to do with those very significant recommendations made by the Knowledge Commission?

Shrimati D. Purandeswari: Sir, as rightly pointed out by the hon. Member, our students have been placed very well globally. For example, 12% of the scientists in the United States are Indians. We have 38% of the doctors in the U.S. who are again Indians. 36% of the NASA scientists are again Indians. So, the students are doing very well, and they are reaching places which again reflects on the quality of education that is being provided to our children in our country.

The very next morning *The Times of India* reported the exchange and Minister Puradneswari's data with great enthusiasm:

36% of scientists at NASA are Indians: Govt survey
NEW DELHI: If you thought that Global Indian Takeover was just a hollow cliche leaning on a few iconic successes like Pepsi's Indra Nooyi, Citibank's Vikram Pandit and steel world's Lakshmi Mittal, there is a slew of statistics now to give it solid ballast.

The extent to which desis have made an impact in the US was reeled off in the Rajya Sabha—as many as 12% scientists and 38% doctors in the US are Indians, and in NASA, 36% or almost 4 out of 10 scientists are Indians.

If that's not proof enough of Indian scientific and corporate prowess, digest this: 34% employees at Microsoft, 28% at IBM, 17% at Intel and 13% at Xerox are Indians.[6]

---

[6]Akshaya Mukul, '36% of Scientists at NASA are Indians: Govt Survey', *The Times of India*, 11 March 2008.

The throbbing enthusiasm lasted for exactly twenty-four hours. The very next day, *The Times of India* published another report:

India rising in US: Govt falls victim to net hoax
WASHINGTON: It's an Internet myth that has taken on a life of its own. No matter how often you slay this phony legend, it keeps popping up again like some hydra-headed beast.

But on Monday, the Indian government itself consecrated the oft-circulated fiction as fact in Parliament, possibly laying itself open to a breach of privilege. By relaying to Rajya Sabha members (as reported in *The Times of India*) a host of unsubstantiated and inflated figures about Indian professionals in US, the government also made a laughing stock of itself.

The figures provided by the Minister of State for Human Resource Development Purandeshwari included claims that 38% of doctors in [the] US are Indians, as are 36% of NASA scientists and 34% of Microsoft employees.

There is no survey that establishes these numbers, and absent a government clarification, it appears that the figures come from a shop-worn Internet chain mail that has been in circulation for many years. Spam has finally found its way into the Indian Parliament dressed up as fact.[7]

As Abraham Lincoln once famously tweeted: 'You can't make this stuff up.'

Publishing dubious potted history on your blog is one thing. But reading out the most hackneyed email forward in Independent India's history in Parliament, and thereby recording your inability to tell fact from froth in perpetuity, is a completely different, hilarious thing. Especially if you're a minister of state.

[7]Chidanand Rajghatta, 'India Rising in US: Govt Falls Victim to Net Hoax', *The Times of India*, 12 March 2008.

Dwell also for a moment on the two stories that appeared in *The Times of India*. Note that some of the 'facts' reported in the first story weren't mentioned by the minister at all. The minister said nothing at all about the proportion of staff at IBM, Intel or Xerox that are Indians. The newspaper embellished the original story with these facts and then promptly washed their hands off it in the second report. After conveniently foisting blame on a 'shop-worn Internet chain'.

How many such internet myths are out there? Why do so many people take them at face value? More importantly, which of these are true?

These questions wouldn't be so germane if only the odd uninformed minister or effervescent retired judge threw around these 'India facts' now and then. In fact, some of these potted, pre-packaged notions of Indian greatness have deeply seeped into popular culture as well.

❋᭱❋

One of the biggest Hindi film hits of 2007 was the Akshay Kumar and Katrina Kaif starrer *Namastey London*. The film grossed some $15 million internationally, and told the story of a British-Indian girl who is forcibly married off to a lovable country bumpkin from Lassi Road, Bumpkinpur, North India. The couple returns to London. Immediately, the girl rejects her marriage and tells Akshay Kumar that she intends to leave him and marry her English boyfriend.

She flies back to London only to be subjected to terrible racism by the English. Which drives her into the arms of her bumpkin bumchum. Perhaps the most popular scene in the film is the one in which Akshay Kumar's character 'humbly' reminds a racist British man of India's achievements:

Akshay Kumar: Mr Pringle, I'd like to tell you something about India. When we greet one another, we fold our hands in namastey, because we believe that God resides in the heart of every human being.

We come from a nation where we allow a lady of Catholic origin to step aside for a Sikh to be sworn in as Prime Minister and a Muslim President to govern a nation of over 80 per cent Hindus.

It may also interest you to know that many of the origins to your words come from Sanskrit. For example, *maatr* becomes mother, *bhratr* becomes brother, *giamiti* becomes geometry, *trikonniti* becomes trigonometry.

We have 5,600 newspapers, magazines in over twenty-one different languages, with a combined readership of over 120 million.

We have reached the moon and back, yet you people feel that we've only reached as far as the Indian rope trick.

We are the third largest pool in the world of doctors, engineers and scientists.

Maybe your grandfather didn't tell you that we have the third largest army in the world.

And even then, I fold my hands in humility before you because we don't believe we are above or beneath any individual.

Namastey.

Katrina Kaif: [I want to have this man's babies at the earliest possible date.]

This script excerpt doesn't really do justice to the simultaneous awfulness and awesomeness of this scene. It is clever, manipulative filmmaking that you feel instantly guilty about enjoying. It is, in other words, the Bollywood equivalent of a chocolate-dough pizza topped with Nutella, banana and whipped cream. With Diet Coke.

The thing about all these 'India facts'—spouted by judges, ministers and film stars—is that many of them are quite possibly false. Many of them are also quite possibly true. But which ones? Are 36 per cent of all NASA scientists really Indians? Did 'giamiti' really become geometry? Who is Sushruta? Did he really invent plastic surgery? There are British people still called Pringle?

Yet, the shaky legitimacy of these claims hasn't prevented them from proliferating like an information pop-culture Ebola virus. References to this long, ever-growing, ever-changing canon of India's greatness keep popping up everywhere, from Parliament to Bollywood. An Indian Independence Day or Republic Day holiday isn't complete unless someone—a friend, a colleague, a retired relative with too much free time—sends you an email or an SMS or a WhatsApp message titled '60 Reasons You Should Be Proud You Are an Indian'.

For years I have received these emails and messages. For years I would laugh them off as some gullible patriot's harmless display of pride. For years I didn't think these lists merited more than a glance, a chuckle-and-delete. After all, it is not as if everyone who shouts 'East or West, India Is the Best' at a cricket match actually thinks of that as a justifiable ideological position.

Then, six years ago, I became a full-time journalist. I began working with *Mint*, a major national business daily. In the course of my job, I began to realize that some of the smartest, most educated, most influential people in the country believed in these 'facts' blindly. So blindly, and so fervently, that many wouldn't even harbour the idea of weighing the veracity of these perceptions.

I once interviewed a very senior advisor to the government who insisted that his goal was to return India to its pre-colonial glory. I asked him why he thought that things in India were glorious before the Empire. He said, 'Everybody knows that before the British came we were the richest country in the world.'

Over the years, I've seen this happen over and over again. In casual conversation, during meetings and during business and policy presentations, facts from these lists would be referred to in passing. Most of the audience would nod along in agreement.

Which in itself isn't really a problem. A little ignorance is admissible in even the highest circles of government. In fact, it is often advisable. But this unquestioning trust in urban legend, as it were, becomes a problem when your Minister of State for Higher Education cites the most dubious statistics as justification of India's educational system. This is when you begin to wonder: How far does this rabbit hole of instant jingoism go? How many policies are made, positions are taken and decisions are executed in complete ignorance of historical truth?

Slowly, I began to see these inaccuracies everywhere. In January 2013, I landed at an airport in India (I think it was Mumbai airport), and as I waited for my bag to bounce along on the conveyor belt I noticed a massive poster on the wall emblazoned with a quote: 'Be the change you want to see.' Underneath was printed the name of the utterer of these immortal words: Mahatma Gandhi.

Unfortunately, Gandhi actually never said those words. As a 2011 op-ed column[8] in *The New York Times* explains, the closest Gandhi got to saying anything similar was: 'If we could change ourselves, the tendencies in the world would also change. As a man changes his own nature, so does the attitude of the world change towards him… We need not wait to see what others do.'

[8]Brian Morton, 'Falser Words Were Never Spoken', *The New York Times*, 29 August 2011.

Almost. But not quite the pithy one-liner on the airport wall. Yet, this is one of Gandhi's most popular 'quotes'.

Why are we so easily swayed by facts forwarded by email? Why do so many Indians believe that the Taj Mahal was originally a temple called Tejo Mahalaya? Why do so many of us instantly believe and immediately proselytize that 'India has never invaded any country in her last 1,000 years of history' or that 'The word "navigation" is derived from the Sanskrit *navgath*' without even pausing to ask: 'Is any of this actually true?'

That may be the natural question. But it is a tough question to answer.

Instead, I decided, I was going to ask a bunch of simpler questions. Questions that, hopefully, would have simpler answers.

I was going to find out which of a handful of the most popular, oft-repeated 'India facts' were actually true. How many of them are rooted in reality? How many of them are make-believe?

This book is the end-product of a year-long pursuit of truth. At the end of this whole exercise, I learnt—as you will shortly—that India actually has, kind of, invaded other countries. That plastic surgery was, kind of, invented in India. And that, among other things, India both invented the zero and didn't invent the zero.

History, it turns out, is more complicated and interesting than it looks.

ONE

A Curious Chirurgical Operation

The first periodical in the world to call itself a 'magazine' was *The Gentleman's Magazine* founded in London in 1731. Edward Cave, its founder, named it after the French word 'magazine', meaning storehouse. And what a storehouse of news, views, information, gossip and reportage *The Gentleman's Magazine* was! Indeed, many people consider it the first general interest magazine ever published.

Right from the get go, *The Gentleman's Magazine* blazed a trail that almost every other magazine in history has since traversed on: It launched with great aplomb, it was marketed and distributed astutely, it employed some great writers and, like every bloody magazine in the world, it eventually began to lose money and ran itself into the ground. (And this was even before the Internet. Which only goes to show that there has always been a general lack of interest in general interest.) Still, credit must be given where it is due. The publishers of *The Gentleman's Magazine* somehow kept the title afloat for almost two centuries. The last issue was printed in 1922. By then it was just a pitiable four pages long.

The publication was distinctly a product of its time—the age of enlightenment. This period from the late-seventeenth to the late-eighteenth century was one of great scepticism, scientific inquiry and popular curiosity in Europe. *The Gentleman's Magazine*, therefore, was always packed with curious stories and wondrous things from all over the known world. And the edition of October 1794 told a particularly strange story from a foreign land. A story that has since passed into the annals of medical history, but not without controversy.

The first clue as to why this particular issue of the magazine has been a perpetual talking point lies in the full-page illustrations that accompanied the closely printed pages that formed the bulk of the issue. Each issue of *The Gentleman's Magazine* came with a few pictures, and the October 1794 edition was embellished with three. Two were unremarkable: a 'Picturesque view of Lullintgon Church, in Somersetshire', and one page of 'Accurate plans of the keeps of Chilham and Canterbury Castles'.

The third was something quite different: 'A portrait illustrative of a remarkable chirurgical operation'.

The illustration features a Maratha man called Cowasjee. Cowasjee looks quite splendid in it. He is dark, lean and quite muscular. He wears a turban and is bare-chested except for a cloth over one shoulder. He also has the doleful eyes of a St. Bernard. None of which was the reason for his inclusion in the issue. What earned Cowasjee a place in the issue was the fact that he been subject to a successful rhinoplasty operation. In 1794, at a time when European surgeons were still struggling with grafting skin from one place of the body to another, Cowasjee had had a nose job done. Not in the great university cities of Western Europe, or at the hands of a royal physician at one of the world's many royal courts. But at the hands of a roadside surgeon, perhaps even a part-time one, in Pune.

A few pages after the portrait is the despatch from India that the engraving of Cowasjee is meant to illustrate. According to this dispatch, two British doctors Thomas Cruso and James

Trindlay, witnessed Cowasjee's rhinoplasty operation first hand in Pune.

Cowasjee's nasal condition, the despatch says, originated in the Third Anglo-Mysore War in which he drove a bullock-cart for the English. Captured by Tipu Sultan's forces, Cowasjee had one hand and his nose cut off—this being well before the Geneva Convention. For a year, the article said, Cowasjee lived in this noseless state before he went to Pune to obtain a new one from a 'man of the Brickmaker cast'.

Cruso and Trindlay watched enraptured as the 'surgeon' first made a thin cast of Cowasjee's missing nose from a piece of wax. He then flattened out the piece of wax, flipped it upside down and laid it against Cowasjee's forehead[9].

> A line is drawn around the wax, and the operator then dissects off as much skin as it covered, leaving undivided a small slip between the eyes. This slip preserves the circulation till a union has taken place between the new and old parts.

This flap of skin is then pulled forward, over the missing nose, and draped onto a scaffold of cloth and cotton to keep the nostrils open. It is then bound up with a poultice of herbs and allowed to heal. A few days later...et voila! New nose. The story concludes with the words: 'This operation is very generally successful.'

To this day, there is much controversy surrounding every single aspect of the Cowasjee story in *The Gentleman's Magazine*. There are disagreements about its authorship, about the names of the two doctors who witnessed the operation, and if they actually ever witnessed this operation at all. Even as recently as

---

[9] *The Gentleman's Magazine*, LXIV, pt. 2, no. 4, October 1794, pp. 891-92, 1 plate, 8vo.

2009, articles in medical journals were debating the provenance of the Cowasjee story.

But one thing is beyond dispute: the Cowasjee story of October 1794 set in motion a series of events that changed medical science forever. Its impact was so immediate and so widespread that it is considered a milestone in the history of European surgery in general, and plastic surgery in particular.

Do remember that this was a time when rhinoplasty—or nasal reconstruction—was something of a nascent procedure in Europe. Surgeons all over the continent were still struggling with problems such as shaping the nose properly and keeping the skin graft alive. The latter was a particularly challenging conundrum.

As anybody who has hacked off large parts of his or her body for leisure will testify, as soon as a piece of flesh is separated from the circulatory system it begins to die. Therefore, while surgeons were perfectly capable of sculpting out perfect skin grafts from cheeks or thighs, these grafts began to die even before they had been sown into the patient's half-nose.

But lo and behold! This kumhar, or brickmaker, from Pune was sowing noses back on to the faces of Indians willy-nilly. What surprised European readers most, perhaps, was the brickmaker's technique for keeping the graft alive: he never severed it from the body at all. A tiny slip of skin anchored the flap folded back from the forehead to the nose. And this kept it alive, nourishing the flap with blood whilst it bonded onto the nose. Once the bond was complete, the flap was trimmed out leaving a perfectly reformed nose. Kind of.

The method was utter simplicity itself. Sure, you'd have a little scar on your forehead. But at least you had a nose that wouldn't fall off awkwardly in the middle of a waltz or a fox hunt or some hearty guillotining or whatever it is that posh Europeans did at the time. Europeans, charmed by the technique and cognizant of its provenance, called this method of rhinoplasty the Hindu or Indian method. And it became a springboard from which a whole range of surgical innovations were launched in the subsequent years.

The Cowasjee despatch is the kind of magazine story that all journalists want to write. The kind of story that surprises and excites and provokes intense discussion. The kind of story that changes something forever. How many times have I rummaged through archives, massaged spreadsheets and played Angry Birds in libraries…all for that one epochal news nugget that will change the world forever.

But what made the story epochal? Why did it turn European surgery on its head? What was that brickmaker of Pune doing that took Europe by surprise?

As it turns out, not a lot. There is a distinct possibility that Europeans had already heard of Indian surgery before. Many now believe that at least a handful of European surgeons in the sixteenth century were familiar with the works of an insurmountable titan of Indian medical and surgical history. What Cowasjee's story did was not, in fact, reveal a new technique to the Western world. Instead, it had revived knowledge that had once wound its way westwards from the east in the form of an ancient compendium of scientific thought, but had then been forgotten.

Indeed, this ancient book of medicine and surgery had a tendency of getting lost and then found and then lost again. In this regard, it was much like its author—a man credited with some of ancient India's greatest intellectual achievements. And an 'India fact' in his own right.

The accomplishments of that brickmaker of Pune that excited Europe so much were but the fruits of this man's pioneering discourses.

That man, the real hero of our story, is the so-called 'father of plastic surgery', Sushruta. And his path-breaking body of work on medical science, often credited with spreading the wisdom of ancient Indian surgery, was the *Sushruta Samhita*.

But was he really the father of plastic surgery? How much of all this is true?

彩彩彩

On 4 July 1990, whilst the Vadukut family was driving to Abu Dhabi airport to catch a flight and embark on its annual month-long vacation in India, my mother had a heart attack. It happened in that freakish, unexplainable way that you find amusing when it happens to other people but baffling when it happens to yourself.

My father, and his entire universe, immediately fell to pieces. My brother was much too young to grasp the significance of all of this. I was just about old enough to understand death but still young enough to withdraw conveniently into an imaginary happy place in my mind. One thing led to another, and I was enrolled in a boarding school—where I would spend a couple of years whilst my dad got his life back into a semblance of order and cheer and normalcy.

The point of telling you this story is to explain how a perfectly healthy, if somewhat flabby, young boy living in Abu Dhabi suddenly ended up sprawled on the ground by a badminton court in a boarding school in Kerala, hyperventilating to within an inch of his life.

Asthma was one of the many things I discovered in those two years in boarding school. Along with field hockey, prickly heat powder, how to dress and undress in public within the purdah of a bath towel wrapped around your waist, and masturbation.

During my very first evening sports session at the boarding school, one of the wardens insisted that I leap into a game of dodgeball—we called it squareball—with gusto.

I tried to reason with the man. 'Look, sir,' I said, 'I was brought up to be a man of letters, high thinking and fine dining. You want a quickly composed limerick or haiku? Look no further than this shivering mass of self-consciousness in front of you. But ducking volleyballs thrown at your face by barbarian wolf-children? No, sir. A thousand times no!'

He was unmoved. Fifteen or twenty minutes later, I had collapsed on the ground, gasping for air. I'd just been battered, bruised, insulted, laughed at and chased around the playing field to the very limits of weak, NRI cardiac capacity. There were large volleyball-shaped welts all over my body. (To this day, when I am bathing vigorously, or undergoing a massage of some kind, I find the word 'Mikasa' imprinted in my most intimate regions.)

For two hours, maybe more, nobody paid any attention. And then one of the Catholic priests who ran the boarding school called home and told them to take me away.

'Welcome, my son,' my grandfather said when we reached home, 'welcome to the sacred brotherhood of asthmatics on your mother's side of the family.' He said it with real pride. People inherit all kinds of things from their parents. Some people inherit sharp aquiline features, speedy metabolism and vintage Swiss watches. I inherited a coconut orchard with space for ninety-six palms from my father's side. And chunky legs, a hairy back and asthma from my mother's side.

The next six or seven years of my life were punctuated by periodic asthma attacks, and all kinds of bizarre experimental treatments to rid me of the wretched disease.

Nothing worked.

Until, when I was about eighteen years old, an aunt dragged me along to visit an Ayurvedic doctor who had suddenly become a la mode. (Is this a peculiarly Kerala thing? Or is it just that my extended family is full of gullible hypochondriacs? Every few months, the Vadukuts would suddenly be raving about 'some new fellow in Kechery who can heal any form of skin condition' or a new 'wizard of the varicose veins in Vadakkanchery'. Immediately, taxis would be hired and an assortment of hypochondriacs, young and old, would rush for medical attention.)

Apparently this Ayurvedic fellow was the arch nemesis of all complaints of the respiratory system. His remedies were simple, his prices low and his word-of-mouth reputation glittering. So, one weekend, we booked a taxi.

The doctor lived in a small, single-storey house inside a gated compound. But his consultations were held in a small shed in the forecourt. It was a tiny little thing that looked like a converted cowshed or scooter garage. The meticulously white-washed shed was split into two sections, a waiting area and a consulting room, separated by a thin, gauzy curtain.

Everything seemed perfectly minimal and efficient and unquack-like, except, perhaps, for the massive framed print hung on the wall of the waiting room.

It was huge. A rectangle at least four feet long and three feet high.

The print was of a vaguely ancient Indian medical scene. Painted in Raja Ravi Varma style, it showed a surgery of the ear in progress. The presiding surgeon, a reed-thin old man with a face engulfed in grey whiskers, sits on cushions at the head of a low bed. On the bed lies a patient, his head turned to one side. The patient seems tranquil, but perhaps not of his own volition. That is because he is being held down by two other men. One holds him down by the legs, the other by the torso. The whole procedure is being watched over by a fourth man and a woman. The woman, who has just stepped into the room, holds a bowl in her hands. She seems poised to swoop down and assist the doctor in some way. All the men are dressed in a simple white dhoti and nothing else. The woman is dressed in a blue blouse and a saffron-coloured sari.

Underneath the massive print was a caption that read something like: 'Susrutha, the father of plastic surgery, in his hospital in 600 BCE.'

That was the first time, as far as I can recall, that I'd ever seen that print. But in the years since, the print has proven to be almost as ubiquitous as the claim that 'Sushrut invented plastic surgery in India centuries before anybody else in the world'.

I've seen reproductions of that print in museums, government offices, airports, textbooks, websites, coffee-table books. And I'm pretty sure I've seen it on a T-shirt.

And while the picture remains constant, the caption is prone to variation. Sometimes it is a picture of 'Sushruta operating on an ear'. At other times, it is a picture of 'A cataract operation'. Sometimes, it is simply a picture of 'Plastic surgery in ancient India'.

This nebulosity is also a common feature of 'India facts' in general. While the general 'fact' gets repeated over and over again, the actual details vary widely.

When I first began cataloguing the themes I wanted to cover in this book, Sushruta's claim to have invented plastic surgery was one of the first that got picked. The ubiquity of that picture played no small part in that choice. I was convinced, in the beginning, that it was a painting completed at some point by an Indian commercial artist and had wound its way into the print market, and then been replicated over and over again. Much like Raja Ravi Varma's *Saraswati* or, internationally, Vladimir Tretchikoff's *Chinese Girl*.

So when I first began researching this chapter, I decided to start with that painting. Was that anorexic old man really supposed to be Sushruta? Who was the artist behind this oft-repeated work? Most importantly, are any of those captions true?

It turns out that the painting wasn't painted by an Indian at all. It was actually commissioned, of all the places in the world, in Michigan in the United States.

In 1948, Michigan-based pharmaceutical giant Parke-Davis commissioned local painter Robert Thom to create a series of eighty-five oil paintings. Forty of these would depict 'Great Moments in Pharmacy', and the other forty-five would depict 'Great Moments in Medicine'. The paintings were meant to be somewhat idealized images of great people and great moments in the history of medical care.

When Thom was done, Parke-Davis prepared sets of reproductions of the paintings and sent them to doctors' offices all over the United States. Some pictures were also placed in medical journals and popular magazines. Because many doctors put them up in their waiting rooms, Robert Thom's works of art quickly attained iconic status. Conveniently for Parke-Davis, the prints also carried the company's branding.

One of these paintings was the famous Sushruta picture. In the 10 August 1959 issue of *Life* magazine, Parke-Davis ran a full-page colour advertisement featuring the Sushruta painting. The caption read: 'Susruta—Surgeon of Old India'. Beneath ran Parke-Davis's advertising copy[10]:

> Plastic surgery, usually regarded as a recent medical advance, was practised thousands of years ago by the Hindu surgeon,

[10]*Life Magazine,* 10 August 1959, p. 12.

Suśruta. Living in a society that punished wrongdoers with physical disfigurement, his restorative skills were greatly in demand. His writings contributed to the spread of Hindu medicine throughout the ancient world.

Somehow, over the next few decades, this picture of Sushruta painted by an American illustrator found its way to India, and to a thousand reproductions, including the one on the wall of my Ayurvedic doctor's waiting room. A picture that was designed to promote a brand of modern pharmaceuticals had miraculously transferred into a poster that was used to promote India's traditional medicine heritage.

(My treatment, by the way, was a triumph. It was revolting to the extreme. Every time I had an attack, I was supposed to drink a concoction of a crushed tablet, juice of a crushed shallot and a few drops of honey. It tasted like the Devil. No. It tasted like the Devil had been blended down with a pint of Guinness and a handful of axle grease. The vile potion eradicated my asthma almost completely. Nowadays, I only get the merest hint of a wheezing attack after long bouts of running, gym sessions or badminton. Which is never.)

Wait. If Parke-Davis was so certain of Sushruta's existence and his mastery of restorative surgery, then why enquire any further?

Not quite. Just bear with me for a few more minutes.

We do know that Parke-Davis asked Robert Thom to base all his paintings on real-life characters and moments in medical science. By some accounts, Thom spent eight years travelling around the world, meticulously researching his subjects down to the clothes they may have worn and the tools they may have used.

It is tempting to draw resolution from Thom's meticulous research. But that wouldn't be the way of Sceptical Patriots would it? We are cut from a tougher, more masochistic length of cloth. So let us figure things out for ourselves, even if this means repeating much of Thom's globetrotting pursuit of truth.

Where do we start?

✳

This chapter features the first of our patriotic pursuits of truth. Here is an opportune moment to talk about the approach this book will take to check the veracity of all these popular 'India facts'. And what it ultimately hopes to achieve.

The primary goal of this book is to evaluate each of these notions of Indian history and see if they stand up to scrutiny. Our secondary goal is to do this with a balanced mix of efficiency and enjoyment. It is entirely possible to write big, fat, fascinating books that investigate the origins of Sushruta, the *Sushruta Samhita* and then trace the transmission of the *Samhita* from east to west across cultures, kingdoms and centuries.

Or to write big, fact, fascinating books that disprove these notions, as the case may be. The histories involved are replete with anecdotes, personalities and incident.

That is not the path we will take in this book. In this book I've sought to investigate each of these ideas in chapters of around 6,000 words each. This means that we will be efficient with our storytelling.

What this definitely does *not* mean is that we will take the path of least resistance. That would need no more than a page or two worth of logically ordered bullet points per fact, with links to relevant sources.

Instead I will try to find short but entertaining paths of investigation that will meander somewhat, through digression and anecdote, but with our goals firmly in sight. Why? Because I don't want this book to become one of those social science textbooks that turned so many of us away from Indian history in our childhood. I want you to enjoy your reading. I want to tell you about interesting things that I found while researching for this book. And I want to give you some idea of the bizarre inter-connectedness of things. (Even if I do sometime sacrifice 'relevance' for 'awesome'.)

This is why you will read about a scandalous British murder case, a Cambodian inscription and Persian taxation policy amongst many other things in a book that is ostensibly about Indian history. Because the stories and their connections were interesting in the writing, and may prove to be so in the reading as well.

In addition, our focus on enjoyable efficiency will also dictate how we frame our questions and direct our investigations. For instance the most comprehensive way to figure out if plastic surgery originated in India is to comb through every single ancient Indian manuscript, find all references to plastic and restorative surgery, and then compare these to every such reference to every other ancient manuscript in the world. And see which one is the oldest. Are the Indian ones the most ancient? Jhingalalaho! Job done.

Are they not? Fabricate some ancient manuscripts, you patriot!

Kidding.

That is the kind of approach that management consultants call 'mutually exclusive and collectively exhaustive'. That is the kind of mind-numbing approach that works when you get paid by the hour.

I don't get paid by the hour. And neither do you, especially not for reading pop-history books.

So what you will see in this chapter, and most of the others, is a slightly more derivative approach to answering these questions.

For instance let us take the 'fact' facing us now: 'Sushruta invented plastic surgery in ancient India, centuries before Europeans.' There are actually several questions here that require answering. Did Sushruta exist? Did he invent plastic surgery? When did the Europeans invent it? Who came first?

Instead of getting mired in answering all of them, we will start with the most basic: Who was Sushruta? What did he know? When did he live? The answers to these questions could enable us to ask further questions. And hopefully we will keep chipping away till we verify this 'India fact'. All the while keeping in mind that Sushruta himself is not that important. We don't care if plastic surgery was invented in ancient India by Bijumon Biryanveetil or Blossom Babykutty. All we want to know is if they did this before anybody, anywhere else.

Now, several references to the origins of plastic surgery, Parke-Davis's advertisement among them, point to the fact that Sushruta was the father of this science. And that the ancient fundamentals of it can be found in Sushruta's great work, the *Sushruta Samhita*.

How accurate is this narrative?

Sushruta may be long lost to the mists of time. Copies of the *Sushruta Samhita*, however, are easily available. And it is in the pages of this document that we shall begin our hunt.

❋⚶❋

The *Sushruta Samhita* is one of ancient India's greatest texts of any kind. Along with the *Charaka Samhita*, it forms one of the two canonical texts of Ayurveda.

Indeed, we know much more about the text itself than

about the author. And therein lies the greatest challenge with certifying, leave alone dating, Sushruta's existence. The text is unquestionably epochal.

But who wrote it? And when?

The Internet abounds with Sushruta narratives. So do a plethora of research papers, books and newspaper articles. But arguably the most riveting, and the most detailed, discussion is to be found in a three-volume English translation of the *Sushruta Samhita* published in 1907. In the introduction to this work, the scholar, translator and commentator Kaviraj Kunja Lala Bhishagratna, dissects every known reference to Sushruta—or *anyone* called Sushruta—in ancient texts.

Poor Bhishagratna clearly had his work cut out. Life in ancient India, he says, was regarded as an illusion[11]. Contemporary histories often talked of the lives of kings and famous men…

> But they were intended more to elucidate or enunciate the doctrines of certain schools of Ethics or Metaphysics than to record any historical fact or event… Hence the utter futility of attempts to explain a historical fact by the light of a votive medal or tablet unearthed perhaps from the ruins of one of our ancient cities. Such an endeavour serves, in most cases, only to make the 'darkness visible' and the confusion more confounded.

In other words, the more you tried to pin down the lives of India's ancients, the more you were prone to lose your way. Still Bhishagratna soldiers on.

The first hurdle in his path is the origin of the *Sushruta Samhita* itself. The version we have today is the end product of at least one major revision of a pre-existing version. That revision

[11]Introduction i, *An English Translation of the Sushruta Samhita*, edited by Kaviraj Kunja Lala Bhishagratna (Calcutta: S.L. Bhaduri, 1907).

and restructuring of the *Sushruta Samhita* was carried out by the great Buddhist philosopher Nagarjuna. Therefore it is nearly impossible to tell how much of the current text is original. And how much has been added to or edited in the *Sushruta Samhita* after its original authorship. Secondly, there are seems to be references to more than one Sushruta in the texts Bhishagratna scrutinized. There are also references to a certain Sushruta in the Mahabharata, but once again it is unclear if that refers to this same Sushruta or to someone else. Or if the reference is an addition by a later writer or editor, who sought to slightly massage the truth in order to create historical narratives.

After much cross-referencing and analysis, Bhishagratna finally suggests that the *Sushruta Samhita* was written two centuries before the birth of the Buddha. Which implies that the author of the first edition of the Samhita lived around 800 BCE.[12]

As with every other element in this historical puzzle, there are those who disagree with Bhishagratna. Some historians suggest that the Buddha's birth and ministry was followed by a period of great vitality in Indian thinking and science. Therefore, in their opinion, the groundbreaking *Sushruta Samhita* could only have been written during or just after the life of Buddha, when intellectual life bloomed in the region. This approach places Sushruta's life around 600 BCE.

Thus, the closest we can really get to pinning down the era of the *Sushruta Samhita* is a broad chunk of time spanning two centuries.

Which is, all said and done, pretty fuzzy. Also, this brings us no closer to dating the life of Sushruta with any accuracy. Dating the Samhita is one thing. Dating Sushruta's life is an

---

[12]I am going by the dates suggested by the most recent excavations in Nepal, as mentioned in the previous chapter.

entirely different problem. What if the original compilation was completed not by Sushruta but by a student or a disciple immediately after his life…or centuries afterwards? And what if Sushruta was not a real person at all but a mythical personality who was credited with this huge body of work as some sort of quasi religious dedication?

That latter point might sound ludicrous at first glance. But imagine this scenario: Thousands of years from now, archaeologists dig up an old bookstore in the ruins of a twenty-second century human inhabitation that was abandoned by its residents after its infrastructure fell apart and it was overcome by crime, filth and gang wars. Gurgaon, basically. They dig up this bookstore and manage to find a book, of which only a few pages remain intact: 'Leadership lessons from the life of Shaktimaan'.

Now imagine that these few intact but undated pages are from the middle of the book, and therefore give no impression at all that Shaktimaan is a fictional character from Indian television. Also consider that these humans from the future have no other references to Shaktimaan in any of their other archives.

It is not inconceivable to me that these future fellows take these archaeological findings at face value. They may even assume that Shaktimaan was some kind of management guru who was revered by the ancients of Gurgaon.

The point I am trying to make here is that dating the *Sushruta Samhita* does not necessarily have to help us date or even verify Sushruta's existence.

Turn this line of thinking on its head, however, and we have a slightly more useful process of investigation. What if we found a mention of Sushruta in an original dated manuscript? And what if we find this in a medical manuscript of some sort? This would give us a concrete sense of a time period in antiquity when 'Sushruta the healer' was a bonafide notion amongst the ancients.

To go back to our previous analogy, assume those future excavators of Gurgaon were to now find a second reference to Shaktimaan—a scrap of *The Times of India* dating from 2007 CE. Perhaps an episode guide or show note that mentions the character and his super abilities. These future researchers can now safely suggest that both these artifacts—the scrap of newspaper and the pages from the book—both date back to roughly the same time period—around 2007 CE. And they both refer to a person with some repertoire of skills and abilities. Was this person real? Fictional? They can't tell. But this Shaktimaan was well known enough to appear in to unrelated, yet contemporaneous texts.

The trick, then, is to find a manuscript of provable antiquity that mentions Sushruta, preferably in a medical context. Then use that to arrive at a ballpark date for the *Samhita*. Alternately, we could find an old enough copy of the *Samhita*, use that to guess at when Sushruta lived, and then compare that to the emergence of plastic surgery in the West. Both of which work, provided the *Samhita* mentions plastic surgery in some rudimentary form.

The problem with ancient Indian documents is that the oldest of them don't actually go back very far at all. To put things in perspective: The oldest known physical copy we have of the Rig Veda is likely to be the collection of manuscripts held at the Bhandarkar Oriental Research Institute, Pune, that has been dated to 1464 CE. This makes it around three thousand years younger than the Rig Veda itself, a truly mind-boggling indicator of the vintage of these works and the discontinuity in documentary records. The oldest manuscript of any kind found in India is the *Gilgit Lotus Sutra* that is currently held at the National Archives in Delhi and dates back to between the fifth and sixth centuries CE.

Which is still, if you recall, over a millennium after the

Sushruta Samhita is believed to have been written. This leaves us in something of a quandary. We simply don't have original documents that are old enough.

There is historical evidence that by the sixteenth century CE, surgeons in Italy had begun experimenting with skin grafts and nose jobs. Modern researchers suggest that these experimental treatments were popular in Italy but never really caught the fancy of the rest of the continent. (One reason could have been the lack of any anaesthesia that could dull the pain of the surgery.) Indeed the techniques would fall out of fashion for several decades before interest was revived in them thanks to the Cowasjee despatch.

Assuming that the *Samhita* does talk about restorative surgery—and we will come to that later—our immediate challenge then is to date it at least before the Italians began working with skin grafts and prosthetic noses. Can we possibly find any document that mentions Sushruta or the *Samhita* that predates these Italians?

It is clear from Bhishagratna's book that at the time of his writing it in 1907, he was not aware of any such source.

In fact, there was a such a source. And it had been found in the most bizarre circumstances, years before Bhishagratna had published his magnum opus. Then for many years it lay undeciphered. This manuscript, one of the greatest Indian archaeological discoveries of the nineteenth century, suddenly answered a lot of questions.

❊

The Bower manuscript itself has become a landmark in Indian history. But the story of its finding would make any Bollywood thriller go green in the...err, reel with envy.

The story begins, of course, with a treacherous murder near the Karakoram pass. The victim was Andrew Dalgleish, a Scottish merchant operating around Leh and trading goods across the Karakoram. Dalgleish was also quite possibly a part-time British spy. This was the time of the Great Game, when Central Asia bristled with British and Russian spies trying to outwit each other for regional dominance. The British were terrified that the Russians were trying to wheedle their way into India, while the Russians were terrified that they weren't terrifying the British sufficiently.

Dalgleish's murderer was a bankrupt Pathan trader named Dad Mahomed.

Hamilton Bower, who found the manuscript and after whom it was named, described what happened in a travelogue published in 1895:

> At the end of March 1888, Dalgleish, accompanied by some Andyani pilgrims and Boti servants, left Leh for Yarkand. Some distance out, they were joined by Dad Mahomed, and on the fifth day after he had joined them, viz. April 8, 1888, they crossed the Karakorum pass. Dalgleish, who was ahead of the others, crossed first, and just under the crest of the pass trod down a place in the snow and pitched his tent, after which he had his tea. Just as he had finished, the rest arrived, and having taken his advice as to a suitable place, pitched theirs, and then got their tea ready. While they were drinking it, Dalgleish went to their tent. They rose up, and asked him to sit down and have some. He excused himself from drinking any tea, saying he had already had his, but sat down amongst them, and said he would take a little bit of bread to show that there was no ill feeling.[13]

[13]Captain H. Bower, 'A Trip to Turkistan', in *The Geographical Journal* (Including the Proceedings of the Royal Geographical Society), vol. V, January to June 1895, pp. 240-57.

Dalgleish then proceeded to give Mahomed some well-meaning advice on getting his finances in order. Mahomed did not seem to have received this very well.

Shortly after this Dad Mahomed rose. Dalgleish asked him where he was going. He said, 'I will be back directly,' and went out. He then went and got his gun, and coming behind the place where Dalgleish was sitting, fired through the tent. Dalgleish, struck through the right shoulder, uttered a cry, staggered forward and endeavoured to escape to his tent where his arms were; but his assailant interposed, attacking him with a sword. Dalgleish did all that an unarmed man could do, endeavouring to close, and even seizing the sword-blade between his hands; but what could an unarmed do against an armed man? The only thing that delayed the inevitable result was the thick clothes Dalgleish had on, and the difficulty of cutting to effect through them. At last Dalgleish fell on his face in the snow, and Dad Mahomed, standing over him, continued hacking till all was still. The Botis and Andyanis, terrified, stood looking on, and did not come to the rescue, though Dalgleish's dog showed them an example, and gave them an opportunity by seizing the murderer by the leg.

After the murder Dad Mahomed made Dalgleish's servant prepare a meal for him, and then quietly went to sleep on his victim's bed, first making the Andyanis swear, on what purported to be a Koran, that they would not tell what they had seen. But as one of them told me, 'We swore with our lips, but in our hearts we said we would.' The Botis wanted to return to Leh, but the murderer made them go several marches further on, and then cut off their pigtails and told them to be off. As they retired, he fired several shots at them to quicken their movements.

The dastardly Dad Mahomed then disappeared.

The next summer, the British government despatched army intelligence officer Hamilton Bower to the region with a simple mission. Somewhere in the vastness of Central Asia, the vile murderer Dad Mahomed hid. Perhaps with Russian connivance. All Bower had to do was to find him and bring him back.

Bower immediately embarked on this, the most vague assignment thinkable, with alacrity. His pursuit brought him to the village of Kuchar in modern-day China. Bower later recalled:

> As nothing had been heard of the man answering to the description of Dad Mahomed from Bugur, I returned to Kuchar by the main road running at the foot of the Tian Shan mountains, whose snowy peaks could be seen rising up above the haze that seems ever present in Turkistan.
>
> At Kuchar, where I halted for several days, a Turki who had been in India used to come and sit with me in my room in the straw. One day in conversation he told me about an ancient city he knew of built underground in the desert. I thought at first that he meant one of the ordinary buried cities of the Gobi Desert; but he insisted that it was something quite different, and explained that it was underground by the wish of the people that made it, not by reason of a sandstorm. He told me, also, that he and one of his friends had gone there and dug for buried treasure, but had found nothing except a book, I asked to see it, and, going away, he returned in about an hour, bringing some sheets of birch bark covered with writing in a Sanscritic character and held together by two boards. I bought them from him, and it was fortunate I did so, as they have since excited a considerable amount of interest in the learned world...

Eventually, Hamilton Bower managed to track down Dad Mahomed and arrest him. Only for Mahomed to hang himself in his prison cell before he could be brought back to India to be tried. But the success of Bower's original mission was quickly forgotten. Indeed, it was completely eclipsed by the implications of the manuscript Bower found/bought/stole in Kuchar. (There are several theories about how exactly Bower acquired it, few of them laudatory.)

Bower sent the manuscript to the Asiatic Society of Bengal, which at the time served as something of a clearing house for explorers, historians, archaeologists and all the other manifestations of nineteenth-century Indology. The manuscript baffled the Society's experts. Mainly because they couldn't read a word of it. It was a written in a language they had never seen before.

To make sense of it, therefore, someone had to first decode it and then read it. And that unenviable job was enthusiastically taken up by a fascinating character called Augustus Frederic Rudolf Hoernle.

Hoernle was born to a family of German missionaries in Secunderabad in 1841. He was then educated in Germany, Switzerland and finally England. By now ordained into the priesthood, Hoernle spent an extra year in England studying Sanskrit at University College, London. Little wonder then that soon after returning to India, Hoernle switched from teaching the gospel to teaching Sanskrit and philosophy at the Jay Narayan College in Benares. It was there that Hoernle developed a relationship with the great spiritualist and reformer Dayanand Saraswati, about whom he wrote a book, Hoernle's first one.

By the time the *Bower Manuscript* had arrived in Calcutta, Hoernle was principal of the Calcutta Madrasa. In addition, the British government had appointed him to look at all the manuscripts and archaeological finds arising from Central Asia. Which is how the *Bower Manuscript* fell into his hands and became something of an obsession for the rest of his life. Over the next decade, Hoernle began to decipher, translate and analyse the manuscript. And he began publishing excerpts in instalments starting from the mid-1890s. (Too late, no doubt, for Bhishagratna to incorporate into his *Samhita*.)

Hoernle arrived at the conclusion that it dated from around the late fourth or early fifth century CE. More recent scholarship suggests that it dates from around 650 CE.

It doesn't matter which date you go with. Either way, the *Bower Manuscript* was a milestone. At the time it was the oldest Indian document ever found in India. (The *Gilgit Lotus Sutra* was discovered half a century later.) And it led to a stampede of explorers, archaeologists and even document forgers pouring into Central Asia. (Later in his career, Hoernle would find himself in a spot of bother after inadvertently authenticating a cachet of forged documents. There is little to suggest that Hoernle did this with malicious intent, and the *Bower Manuscript* was not one of these contentious documents.)

The manuscript itself, Hoernle found, was a collection of seven texts. Two were guides to fortune-telling, two were descriptions of Buddhist rituals and three were ancient medical manuals. Medicals manuals of great sophistication.

The June 1895 issue of *The British Medical Journal* had a brief note on the finding subtitled 'The Most Ancient Sanskrit Medical Treatise Extant'.

The note outlines some of the contents of the medical manuals: formulae for powders, medicated ghee and medicated oils; formulae for enemas, aphrodisiacs and hair washes; and treatments for children, barren women, and women with children.

The editors of the *Journal* seem cautiously impressed:

> No doubt many of the articles of the Hindu materia medica are of important therapeutic character and might with advantage be tested in hospitals; but a collection of complex farragos prescribed according to a fanciful and erroneous pathology is practically useless.[14]

You can almost hear the posh voices squirm.

In one fell swoop, the *Bower Manuscript* confirmed everything that hitherto had been a matter of conjecture. It provided dated, documentary proof that India had a sophisticated medical tradition that went back to at least 650 CE and even much earlier. (After all there is nothing to suggest that medical manuals in the *Bower Manuscript* is a first edition. For all we know it could be a copy of an older original text. Thus potentially dating back this medical knowledge by many years.)

Sadly, the part of the manuscript that were medical manuals is incomplete. The complete document would have been a work of medical genius perhaps unmatched in the ancient world.

There was one more invaluable nugget of information in the manuscript.

In the opening chapter, the *Bower Manuscript* talked of ten holy men who lived in the Himalayas, with minds of a medical bent. They are called Atreya, Harita, Parasara, Bhela, Garga, Sambavya, Vasistha, Karala, Kapya and, our old friend, Sushruta. The medical manuals of the *Bower Manuscript* prominently quote the works of three of these masters: Charaka, Bhela and Sushruta.

Finally, one of the most popular figures in ancient Indian science had made an appearance in a document of undisputed antiquity.

[14]*British Medical Journal*, June 1895, p. 1216.

By several accounts, the *Bower Manuscript* is the earliest recorded mention of Sushruta the surgeon and physician in a dated document. We can now say with some confidence that at least by 650 CE the ancients knew the teachings of Sushruta, if not Sushruta himself, well enough to quote them in medical compendiums and manuals.

It is now time to take stock of what we've connected so far. So what do we know?

We know that at least by around 650 CE someone called Sushruta was widely held to be one of the great ancient medical scientists, and that some medical knowledge popular in this period was attributed to his body of work. This body of work, the *Sushruta Samhita*, may date as far back as 800 BCE. But must have been widely known at least by 650 CE, in order to merit mention by the authors of the *Bower Manuscript*.

We also know, thanks to the manuals in the *Bower Manuscript*, that by 650 CE, India already had a sophisticated understanding of disease and medicine. So would it be surprising to know that they also knew advanced surgical techniques? Not entirely.

But what did they know? And how good were they at constructing prosthetic noses?

The *Sushruta Samhita* is, to put it mildly, mind-blowing. It is astonishing that while the existence of this text is taught to most Indian school children, the contents are often ignored. It describes, for instance, 76 types of eye-diseases, 121 sharp and blunt instruments used in surgery, 42 surgical processes and 700 plants of medicinal value divided into 37 groups of diseases.

In Chapter 16 of the first book of the *Samhita*, the Sutrasthana, the text outlines a particular surgical process.

> Now I shall deal with the process of affixing an artificial nose.
> First the leaf of a creeper, long and broad enough to fully

cover the whole of the severed or clipped off part, should be gathered; and a patch of living flesh, equal in dimension to the preceding leaf, should be sliced off (from down upward) from the region of the cheek and, after scarifying it with a knife, swiftly adhered to the severed nose. Then the cool-headed physician should steadily tie it up with a bandage decent to look at and perfectly suited to the end for which it has been employed. The physician should make sure that the adhesion of the severed parts has been fully effected and then insert two small pipes into the nostrils to facilitate respiration, and to prevent the adhesioned flesh from hanging down.

Some of the earliest translations of the *Samhita* into English were published starting from the 1830s. But I have chosen this excerpt from Bhishagratna's book.

The similarities to the procedure carried out on Cowasjee are really quite astounding. The only material difference is that the surgeon of Pune grafted skin from the forehead, while the Samhita flipped over a flap of skin from the cheek.

A thousand years or more apart, Indian surgeons were using virtually identical processes of surgery to restore disfigured noses.

Fine. The Cowasjee process was known in India centuries ago. But was it invented in India?

There are two ways of answering this question. First of all, there is some evidence and scholarly commentary to suggest that even the Italian plastic surgeons of the fifteenth and sixteenth centuries who had dabbled in restorative surgery had received at least some of their ideas thanks to Indian medical knowledge being passed on to them through the Arabs. This, again, is a historical investigation unto itself and beyond the scope of this little book. But it is entirely possible that ancient India was the fountainhead of knowledge when it came to restorative surgery.

All roads, as it were, leads back to a particular Indian scientific environment that gave rise to the *Samhita*.

The second way of answering this is by looking at what happened after the Cowasjee despatch was published. An August 2009 piece in the medical journal *Acta Otorhinolaryngol ica Italica* encapsulates this nicely. The Cowasjee despatch, author RC van de Graaf says,

> appears to have fired the imagination of the English surgeon Joseph Constantine Carpue (1764-1846) who initially practiced the Indian method of rhinoplasty on cadavers, and waited until a suitable patient presented himself. Carpue performed his first two rhinoplasties in 1814 and 1815. In 1816, Carpue published the results of these attempts in his landmark work: 'An account of two successful operations for restoring a lost nose from the integuments of the forehead.'

Carl Ferdinand von Graefe (1787-1840) had Carpue's work translated into German in 1817, and subsequently wrote his own book on nasal reconstruction entitled *Rhinoplastik, oder die Kunst den Verlust der Nase organisch zu ersetzen* (1818). The term 'plastic' appears to have been applied to surgery for the first time in history in this publication.

Carpue and von Graefe's work went on to establish rhinoplasty as a legitimate area of enquiry in Europe. And through rhinoplasty, it laid the foundations for the art and science of modern plastic surgery.

So, in a roundabout way spanning millennia, the bricklayer of Pune—and, by extension, the *Sushruta Samhita* and thousands of years of Indian medical heritage—kick-started a revolution in European plastic surgery. Carpue, Von Graefe and their followers built their work on a foundation laid thousands of miles away and thousands of years ago in ancient India.

SCEPTICAL PATRIOT INDIA FACT SCORE CARD

Popular India fact

Sushruta invented plastic surgery in India thousands of years before anybody else.

Score

9/10. While the specifics of the time and place of this invention can never be proven, there is little doubt that by around 650 CE ancient Indian doctors had access to a sophisticated body of medical literature including methods of restorative surgery.

Suggested fact

Ancient Indian doctors were some of the world's first plastic surgeons. They developed techniques that spurred surgical innovations in the nineteenth century.

Homework for the excessively sceptical

1. What if the Cowasjee despatch was a fabrication? There are people who suspect this. Cowasjee, for instance, is a Parsi and not Marathi name. Would this have changed this story drastically?

2. What other historical wonders lay hidden in the lives of Bower, Hoernle, Carpue and Adam Dalgleish?

3. What other pioneering techniques does the *Sushruta Samhita* explain? An English translation seems well worth the investment. There are free ones on the Internet.

3. What happened to medical science in India afterwards? What happened to this wisdom and knowledge? How did the quality of healthcare change in the centuries after the classical period and later?

4. When do we plan a trip to the Bhandarkar Oriental Research Institute in Pune?

TWO

Southern Invaders

For about two and a half centuries, one of the greatest empires in Indian history, and one of the most overlooked in global history, reigned from what is now a tiny village in Tamil Nadu. Eighty kilometres away from Thanjavur, Gangaikondacholapuram is today a small dot on the map known mainly for a spectacular Siva temple—part of a triumvirate of Chola temples that together form a UNESCO World Heritage monument.

Gangaikondacholapuram is quite a mouthful. But it becomes easier to say it once you know what the name stands for: 'The town of the Chola who acquired the Ganga'. But more on that Ganga acquiring business in a bit.

At the height of its imperial power, the Chola Empire directly or indirectly ruled over an area of land estimated at over three and a half million square kilometres. That would make it the seventh largest country in the world today, around half a million square metres—or an entire Spain—bigger than the Republic of India itself.

Almost exactly a thousand years ago, when the Cholas were ruled by their finest emperors, their influence determined the lives of people from Bengal in the north to Sri Lanka in the south, and from Maldives in the west all the way to Java in the east.

Wait! Did I just say Java? Yes. Java. As in Java and Sumatra. As featured in the great disaster film *Krakatoa: East of Java*.

I'm really hoping that this information sends your jaw crashing to the floor and somersaulting out of the door. Yes, an empire based in Tamil Nadu once used to rule over vast chunks of Southeast Asia! (I hope you're not thinking of Java, the computer programming language. That is not the Java I am referring to. Though, of course, many people would say that a vast empire of Tamils, spread out across the world, rules over that other Java too.)

The Cholas were really most remarkable chaps. They were around for a really, *really* long time. And I mean a really long time even by the standards of Indian history. Standards of dynastic durability that are so high that in one of his books, the great historian Abraham Eraly decided to ignore an entire dynasty of South Indian kings because they were only around for some 400 years. Four centuries. A long time for you and me and dogs, but just a rounding-off error in terms of Indian history. Even by those impossible standards, the Cholas enjoyed extraordinary longevity.

The earliest Chola kings we know with any certainty can be dated back to around 300 BCE. Historian Eraly says that our primary source for information on South India of this early period is primarily Greek. Much of this, in turn, was hearsay from traders and merchants. The Greeks referred to the region as Damirica, possibly a corruption of the word Tamizhakam— abode of the Tamils—and had some interesting notions about South Indians. The great Herodotus had this to say about them:

> These Indians whom I have described have intercourse openly like cattle; they are all black-skinned, like the

Ethiopians. Their semen too, which they ejaculate into the women, is not white like other men's, but black like their skin, and resembles in this respect that of the Ethiopians. These Indians dwell far away from the Persians southwards, and were not subjects of King Darius.[15]

How utterly inaccurate. As any resident of the region will tell you, intercourse is not only rare but almost universally forbidden across most of South India. Instead, locals are encouraged to spend their lives in prayer and IIT coaching.

The Chola Empire vanished into the mists of history around 1300 CE, when the last king, Rajendra Chola III, was defeated in battle the arch-rival Pandya dynasty. Which gives the Cholas a historical span of 1,600 years.

Perhaps this will help put this longevity into perspective: You, my reader, live closer in time to Rajendra Chola III than he did to the first Chola kings. Think about that.

The Cholas built superb temples, established sophisticated systems of local administration, simultaneously fended off several local rivals, established trading routes that threaded all the way to ports in China, and left behind an artistic and architectural heritage, remnants of which can be found in museums and collections all over the world.

In short, the Cholas were one of the great Indian empires.

But why should this matter to Sceptical Patriots like you and me, you ask?

This is because the time has come for us to investigate yet another 'India fact'. It is a popular one. And it is the idea that India has never colonized another country in 10,000 years.

The exact wording of this claim changes from Facebook post to Facebook post and blog post to Whatsapp message.

[15]Herodotus, *The Histories* (UK: Penguin, 2003), 3.101.

Sometimes it says *attacked* instead of *colonized*, and 1,000 years instead of 10,000.

But are any of these versions true in any way? Has India never, ever invaded another country?

One spectacular and keenly contested incident in Chola history helps us settle this thorny issue with some satisfaction. The events associated with this great incident unfolded almost exactly a millennium ago. Yet, it was only really understood a generation ago.

Thanks to a single inscription in one of the greatest buildings in India.

※⁂※

There can be no city in India less suited to be a location for an engineering college than Tiruchirapalli—or Trichy, as we used to call it semi-affectionately back in the day. From 1997 to 2001, I spent four glorious years learning metallurgical engineering at the Regional Engineering College, Tiruchirapalli.

I learnt copious quantities of metallurgical engineering, of course, and developed particular proficiency in the study of pitting corrosion properties of austenitic stainless steels. I also matured into a football goalkeeper of passable (pun!) quality, a blogger of middling ability but great enthusiasm, an excellent Bollywood dancer, and a whisky consumer of regional—later, national—repute. It was also in Trichy that I first tasted that cornerstone of North Indian cuisine—paneer.

But, for all these endowments (and a thoroughly well-rounded academic education), Trichy was also one of the most boring places on the planet. No, really. There was *nothing* to do in Trichy. At all. Ever. Anywhere. Why else would I have gone to see *Air Force One* not once but four times in three days when the film first arrived in theatres?

Once, bored out of our skulls and perilously close to throwing ourselves from a rooftop water tank to end our misery, a friend and I went on an epic bus journey to eat chilli beef at the famous Tibetan restaurant in Kodaikanal. We bussed up for four hours, ate for twenty minutes, and then bussed back for four hours. And felt like kings. Chola kings!

It was in this state of constant boredom that we, a group of metallurgical engineering students, decided to go on a leisure trip one weekend to Thanjavur, a temple town a short bus ride way from Trichy.

Leisure trip? Calm down. To be precise, we would depart on a day trip to see the famous Brihadeeswara Temple in Thanjavur. We would go and see the many architectural, cultural and sculptural delights of the temple complex. After this, the God-fearing amongst us would pray at the temple. Then we would rush to an early dinner, surely involving paneer, and then bus back to the campus. We would hopefully return in time for the female members of the leisure trip party to go back to their hostel before lockdown at 8.30 p.m.

All of which was just a cover for a group of well-behaved, conservative South Indian boys and girls to spend a day together, accidentally touching each other's elbows and shoulders and other such erogenous zones, gently accumulating sexual tension, till we all returned to our dorm rooms and exploded spontaneously.

I was myself seeking to impress a particularly comely little thing from Chennai with a husky voice, a high grade point average, delightful handwriting and a reassuringly 'low maintenance' air about her.

But even she, in all her poise and elegance and sizzle, couldn't hold an incense stick up to the awesomeness of the Brihadeeswara Temple. It remains one of the greatest historical buildings of any type I have seen in my life. If you ask me, it deserves to be much, much more popular. However, a lot like the Chola Empire itself, the temple suffers a certain second-class existence.

Even when it was once given its moment in the sun, so to speak, it lasted very briefly. In 1954, the Reserve Bank of India reintroduced high denomination currency notes into circulation. A few years before, the bank had withdrawn 1,000-rupee and 10,000-rupee notes in order to curb 'black'—or large hordes of unaccounted-for—cash. Each of the newly designed high value notes was decorated with the picture of an important historical monument. The 10,000-rupee note was decorated with an image of India's national emblem, the Lion Capital of Ashoka; the 5,000-rupee note had a picture of the Gateway of India in Mumbai; the smallest of the three, the 1,000-rupee note, had a picture of Thanjavur's Brihadeeswara Temple.

Had the note been of a smaller denomination, the temple may have found more widespread mileage. Unfortunately, 1,000 rupees was an astounding sum of money in the 1950s, and it seems unlikely that many Indians noticed the marvel on their big money. To make things worse, in 1978, the Reserve Bank of India decided to withdraw high value notes once again. For exactly the same reason as before.

When the 1,000-rupee note was reintroduced two decades later, it was as part of the new Mahatma Gandhi series. Because, you know, we don't have enough Mahatma Gandhi going around. The curtain was unceremoniously dropped on Brihadeeswara's brief cash cameo.

Even though the temple has lost what might have been its greatest vehicle to widespread popularity, the Brihadeeswara complex still receives thousands of visitors every year. The fact that it is a living, functioning temple helps. Which, when you think about it, is a mind-boggling feat for a building erected over 1,000 years ago.

As we walked around the complex, one of my more well-informed friends narrated certain mysteries and myths associated with the temple. For instance, he told us, many believed that the stone on top of the vimana—the soaring central tower of the temple—used to house an intensely powerful magnet of divine origin. It was so powerful, he said, that it disrupted compasses on boats and ships on the nearby river and even far out at sea. The vimana itself, he continued, housed many such mysterious objects. But during the British colonial period explorers not only broke into the gopuram and stole treasures but they may have removed the super magnet and destroyed it as well.

It is also considered extremely unlucky for politicians to visit the temple—both Indira Gandhi and M.G. Ramachandran died shortly after visiting the complex. Most fascinating of all is a myth that one of the many sculpted human forms on the tower is that of a strangely European-looking character. And this, some say, was a warning by the Cholas of impending foreign invaders (that is, the British).

One feature of the temple, however, is utterly beyond speculation. It is drenched in inscriptions. Find a nice vertical, flat surface of any size in the complex, and odds are that it is covered in carved inscriptions. It was one such inscription that, as recently as half a century ago, took everything we knew about the Cholas and threw it out of the window.

But before we go on a mind-bending Chola investigation, a brief digression on the centrality of inscriptions to understanding Indian history.

Now, two figures from Indian history have a monopoly

over Indian symbols and iconography. The first, of course, is Mahatma Gandhi.

Statues of Mahatma Gandhi—mostly standing, sometimes sitting, often terrible—dot the length and breadth of this great but sometimes unimaginative nation. His portrait adorns the walls of Indian schools, government offices and other institutions. Wikipedia has an exclusive page for 'List of roads named after Mahatma Gandhi'. All manner of things, from engineering colleges to universities to government welfare programmes to a five-a-side football tournament I once played in, have been named after this great man. Oh, and he is all over Indian currency notes as well.

The only other figure that comes even close to emulating Gandhi's ubiquity is the great emperor Ashoka. Obviously we don't see portraits and statues of Ashoka everywhere. Instead, his presence looms over India in the form of the Lion Capital of Sarnath.

When India announced a new Constitution in 1950, the founding fathers and mothers also adopted a new emblem for the republic. This emblem was an adaptation of a sandstone sculpture that once used to cap an inscribed pillar in Sarnath near Benares in Uttar Pradesh. The pillar and capital was erected by Ashoka, it is believed, to celebrate Gautama Buddha's life and teachings. In the six decades since that announcement in 1950, the national emblem—four lions atop a round plinth inscribed with wheels and animal reliefs—has penetrated deep into the lives of Indians everywhere. Thanks to this, perhaps, Ashoka himself has become one of modern India's great historical heroes.

Yet, the astonishing thing is that right up till the middle of the nineteenth century, historians knew nearly nothing about Ashoka or his empire. All that was known about this now legendary king was that he was a patron of Buddhism and a descendant of Chandragupta Maurya. But when it came to details of his reign, the extent of his empire and even the dates of his life, next to nothing was known.

Indeed, some historians doubted if such a king had even existed. There were even talk in some circles (*gasp*) that Ashoka was a legend and nothing more.

All that changed thanks to the relentless hard work and enterprise of an English scholar called James Prinsep. Prinsep travelled all over India collecting and deciphering inscriptions. He was particularly intrigued by identical inscriptions on iron pillars found in places as far apart as Delhi, Allahabad and Bihar. So fervent was Prinsep's efforts that it almost certainly led to his death from exhaustion.

In the beginning, the going was very tough indeed. All attempts at cracking the inscriptions, Prinsep's included, failed. The breakthrough happened in 1837, when an army officer sent Prinsep copies of inscriptions found at an archaeological site at Sanchi near Bhopal. The inscriptions, it turned out, were lists of patrons who had gifted money to build the stupa, or shrine. Prinsep realized that the last word in each line must be 'danam'—gift.

In six weeks, James Prinsep had cracked the Ashoka code. In his fascinating book, *India Discovered*, John Keay explains how this discovery completely rewrote Indian history:[16]

> Suddenly it all began to make sense. Ashoka was already known from the Sanskrit king lists…now his historicity was dramatically established. Thanks to the inscriptions, from being just a doubtful name, more was suddenly known about Ashoka than about any other Indian sovereign before

[16]John Keay, *India Discovered* (New Delhi: HarperCollins, 1988), p. 54.

1100 CE. As heir to Chandragupta it was not surprising that his pillars and inscriptions were so widely scattered. The Mauryan Empire was clearly one of the greatest ever known in India, and here was its noblest scion speaking of life and work through the mists of 2,000 years. It was one of the most exciting moments in the whole story of archaeological discovery.

Prinsep's success was one of those epochal developments that changed a field of human activity completely. It suddenly made other researchers cognizant of the miles of inscriptions that pockmarked derelict temples, ruined palaces and weather-beaten ancient monuments all over India. New groups of scholars began to scour the length and breadth of the colony for insights and moments of Prinsep-like epiphany. And, as these intrepid, often eccentric, Indologists went about their labour, they began to tell a new, mostly unknown history of the subcontinent.

One such inscription hunter was Eugen Julius Theodor Hultzsch. Hultzsch was one of many German Indologists who keep popping up during this period of Indian history. They were not, as one might assume, tourists who landed up in India, fell in love with the country and decided to spend their lives here under the pretence of scholarship or archaeology.

Hultzsch was born in Dresden on 29 March 1857. (Incidentally, this was the exact same day that in Barrackpore near Calcutta, half a world away, an Indian soldier named Mangal Pandey fired the first shots of the great revolt.) After studying Classics and Oriental Languages at the University of Lipsia, Hultzsch moved to Vienna and began working with Georg Bühler, a renowned expert on Sanskrit and Indology.

He became, by all accounts, a complete India nut. Sometime in the early 1880s, Hultzsch visited India for the first time. He toured the north extensively, but eventually decided to move to

Madras. On 21 November 1886, Eugen Hultzsch was appointed as the Government of Madras's epigraphist.

Governments in India are not well known for picking the right guy for the right job. Some of India's most stellar appointments include H.D. Deve Gowda as prime minister, A.K. Antony as defence minister and Sharad Pawar as anything at all. Asking Eugen Hultzsch to locate, record, study and interpret historical inscriptions all over the vast Madras Presidency seems every bit as questionable. Hultzsch's India experience was almost entirely gained in the universities of Germany and Austria. His tour of the north had been intense but short. And, to make things worse, it seemed highly doubtful that temples all over South India would let a magnificently whiskered German infidel to defile their sanctum sanctora. (Some of the most important temples in South India continue to bar non-Hindus from accessing the more central precincts. A few years ago, I visited the Rock Temple in Trichy, where a young priest warned me in no uncertain terms that if they caught any non-Hindus inside, the visitors would have to pay for a very expensive purification ritual. 'Jesus Christ!' I said in shock. Okay, not really.)

Yet, Hultzsch proved to be an inspired appointment, one with lasting resonance through the history, archaeology and epigraphy of South India. Hultzsch took to his job with Teutonic enthusiasm. He toured temple after temple, meticulously copying down inscriptions. Soon he was given a team of dedicated native epigraphists to help him. In later letters and introductions to their books, Hultzsch and company talk of how they ventured into abandoned overgrown temples, slithered into oily, damp caves, and sometimes laid siege on some old temple ruin moments away from demolition, just to copy down the inscriptions. And when Hultzsch was prevented from stepping into any space, his team of natives, many of them Brahmins, did the epigraphy for him.

Driven by the success of people like Prinsep, Hultzsch launched upon monuments such as the Brihadeeswara Temple in Thanjavur with hopes of great findings. And it is within the central shrine of this glorious temple that Hultzsch made one of his most important discoveries.

The temple at Thanjavur was commissioned during the reign of Rajaraja I, the first great emperor of the Cholas. Rajaraja was the kind of guy one of my favourite newspaper editors would call 'a dude'. When he came to the throne around 985 CE, the Cholas were little more than a fledgling power. South India at the time enjoyed a precarious balance of power, with at least three local dynasties battling for supremacy. Indeed, some of Rajaraja's first few battles were against little more than local chieftains and rebellious vassals. By the time his reign had concluded, however, around 1014 CE, the Chola Empire was one of India's strongest and best administered political powers. Rajaraja was also a patron of the arts, especially of the art of temple building. The Brihadeeswara Temple of Thanjavur was his finest architectural achievement.

Besides the length and breadth of his empire, and his endless 'dudeness', there is one more reason we know so much about Rajaraja I. And that is thanks to a new trend in inscriptions that was started by this first great Chola king.

Inscriptions had always been a favourite tool of the kings of the south, especially if they wanted to leave their stamp on a newly conquered kingdom or vassal. Shortly after defeating a villainous enemy and suitably plundering his kingdom, the victorious king would summon his scribes. These chaps would then hammer out a glorious reminder of the victory on a pillar, temple wall or stone surface, conveniently leaving a record for future historians to date events and lives by. (Some say that this was a practice passed on to Indian kings by the Acheamenid kings of Persia.)

But Rajaraja took it one step further. He ordered that his Chola inscribers not only state the matter at hand—a temple was inaugurated here; a battle was won here; my cousin went to Thanjavur and all he got for me was this loincloth—but also that each such inscription, space permitting, must start with a brief profile of the king, complete with a brief selection of his military conquests.

This may have been a pain in the rear end for the poor inscribers. But for later historians, Rajaraja's new trend was all kinds of epigraphic awesome. No doubt there was a healthy dose of hyperbole in these inscriptions, but the list of military conquests that prefaced even mundane inscriptions help them to scope out the lives of other kings, date battles and expeditions, and establish who was doing what and where.

To make things even better, Rajaraja's successor kings stuck to the same inscription protocol. Thus historians can now piece together several aspects of South Indian history by stitching together these little stone profiles.

But all this happened after hard work by epigraphists such as Hultzsch.

From the south wall of the central shrine inside the Thanjavur temple, Hultzsch and his associates copied down an inscription from the reign of Rajendra I, Rajaraja's immediate successor. The main message of the inscription was mundane enough—it ordered the temple to annually grant a measure of rice to a certain priest. However, the introductory portions of that inscription, the bits of glorious profile with the military conquests of Rajendra I, contained a peculiar list of conquests:

> (Who) having despatched many ships in the midst of the
> rolling sea and having caught Sangramavijayottungavarman,
> the king of Kedaram, together with the elephants in his

glorious army, (took) the large heap of treasures, which (that king) had rightfully accumulated; (captured) with noise the (arch called) Vidhyadharatorana at the 'war-gate' of his extensive city; Sri Vijaya with the 'jewelled wicket-gate' adorned with great splendour and the 'gate of large jewels'; Pannai with water in its bathing ghats; the ancient Malaiyur with the strong mountain for its rampart; Mayirudingam, surrounded by the deep sea (as) by a moat; Ilangasoka (i.e., Lankasoka) undaunted (in) fierce battles; Mapappalam having abundant (deep) water as defence; Mevilimbangam having fine walls as defence; Valaippanduru having Vilapanduru; Talaittakkolam praised by great men (versed in) the sciences; Madamalingam, firm in great and fierce battles; Ilamuridesam, whose fierce strength rosin war, Manakkavaram, in whose extensive flower gardens honey was collecting; and Kedaram, of fierce strength, which was protected by the deep sea.

These inscriptions dated to around 1033 CE. They were copied down and published over eight and a half centuries later, in 1891, by Hultzsch. Enough time, surely, for all these places of Cholan conquest—Kedaram, Sri Vijaya, Pannai, Malaiyur—to have been identified, chronicled and excavated.

Far from it. In fact none had even heard of these places, let alone identify where these cities and kingdoms were. Where in the world had Rajendra I been to?

It would take another two decades after Hultzsch's original discovery and translation before someone could conclusively identify these places. But when they were identified, their location stunned historians. It not only made everyone reassess the ambitions of the Cholas, but it also helps us debunk one of the most oft-quoted 'India facts'.

✻✲✻

India was the greatest colony in the history of all colonies anywhere. No other colony made as much money for its masters. No other colony sent so many soldiers to fight wars for its emperor kings. No other colony was ruled with such a sophisticated system of administration. No other colony was so big and so full of subjects. No other colony was so complicated to get in, and so complicated to get out of. No other colony had such enduring implications for the state of the planet. No other colony's current existence has been so impacted by its colonial past. India was the colony to rule over all colonies. (Hah.)

This is why, perhaps, one of the central aspects of the 'India narrative' is its colonial past. When India seeks to explain its frustrating present or uncertain future, it often trawls through its colonial experience. Terrible law and order systems? Blame the British legacy of our penal codes. Too few cities and too many villages? All down to the British and their hideous need to keep people separate. Regional acrimony? Divide-and-rule refuses to go away.

But there is a flip side to this tendency. And that flip side is this great 'India fact': India has never invaded another country in 10,000 years.

After all, how can you ride on a sympathy wave for your oppressed colonial past unless you can prove that you were never a colonial power yourself?

Now, there is plenty to quibble over here. The 'police action' against the State of Hyderabad in 1948, or the invasion of Goa in 1961, have all been referred to as acts of territorial aggression and annexation by certain aggrieved parties.

But weren't they also attempts by a young country to re-establish integrity? Possibly.

Centuries before that, our old friends the Cholas invaded Sri Lanka. Not once but several times. Some of these invasions were brutal affairs complete with rape, pillage and desecration of Buddhist temples. The *Mahavamsa*, Sri Lanka's great historical poem-chronicle, says of one Cholan invasion of around 1017 CE:

> In the three fraternities and in all Lanka (breaking open) the relic chambers, (they carried away) many costly images of gold etc., and while they violently destroyed here and there all the monasteries, like blood-sucking yakkas, they took all the treasures of Lanka for themselves.

In fact, the Cholan colonization of Sri Lanka lasted for several years. But does invading Sri Lanka really count? Surely that was only a regional skirmish?

What could utterly thwart that 'India fact' would be proof that an Indian king attacked and established overlordship over a foreign land far away for motives that were at least partially commercial.

In 1918, a Frenchman proved exactly that.

George Coedes is said to have been born in Paris in 1886. (Maybe he was born exactly around the time Hultzsche was tracing those inscriptions in Thanjavur.) In 1911, he joined the staff of the French Institute for the Far East in Hanoi, Vietnam. Coedes then spent nearly half a century investigating the history of the Malay Peninsula and Java. In particular, he investigated the idea of the 'Indianized kingdom'.

Coedes was convinced that, over time, many of the ancient kingdoms that ruled over parts of modern-day Indonesia, Malaysia, Thailand and Cambodia had slipped under heavy Indian influence. But that is a matter for another controversial book.

Coedes's greatest contribution to the better understanding of the history of this part of the world was his discovery of Sri

Vijaya. The exact mechanics of how he did this is also a matter for another book.

What concerns the Sceptical Patriot is the startling revelation Coedes made in a 1918 memoir titled *Le Royaume de Sri Vijaya*.[17] In this book, Coedes connected the kingdom of Sri Vijaya to, of all the things in the world, the Rajendra I inscription that Hultzsch copied down inside the Thanjavur temple a generation before.

Coedes's research led him to believe that the long list of unknown names in the inscription all referred to places in Burma, the Nicobar Islands, the Malay Peninsula and Java. According to the inscription, Rajendra I had conquered all these places. Coedes went on to say that the Chola navy had not only raided these places but also effectively ruled them as vassals for close to a century.

Minds, as they say, were blown. Think about it. Suddenly the Chola Empire went from being a small but ambitious power in South India to a regional power with an international footprint. This was not a raid of a neighbouring kingdom or an island across a lagoon. It was a full-fledged naval operation across 2,000 miles of mostly-deep ocean.

There was, as you might expect, much outrage and surprise at Coedes's results. But in the years since that original revelation, much of his research has passed muster.

The Thanjavur inscription remains the most important textual proof of the Chola colonies of Sri Vijaya. But other sources have also been forthcoming. Today, researchers have found references to Chola control of the region in Chinese

[17]Georges Coedes, *Le Royaume de Sri Vijaya* (Hanoi: Imprimerie d'Extrême-Orient, 1918).

documents. They also have surprisingly rich information of how the Cholas drew up their navies, financed their expeditions and built their ships. Indeed, some historians believe that the Chola navies were primitive public-private projects, with merchant guilds and trader groups financing the raids.

The one thing that still puzzles historians is why the Chola forces embarked on such an audacious mission. Inscriptions indicate that shortly before the raids, which took place around 1025 CE, the kings of Sri Vijaya maintained friendly relations with the Cholas. It appears that the Sri Vijayan kings even financed the establishment and maintenance of Buddhist temples near modern-day Nagapattinam.

Yet, for some reason that we will probably never know without time travel, the Cholas later sailed over and gave the Sri Vijayans a mighty good spanking. And, as we said before, the conquests remained subservient to the Cholas for around a century.

Squashing a friendly nation does seem like a treacherous kind of thing to do. But various theories for the Chola attacks have been floated. Sri Vijaya controlled the trade routes between India and China. Some historians suggest that the Sri Vijayans may have got too greedy and strangled the shipping routes with taxes and levies. Irate Chola traders may have coaxed the government into action.

In the 1920s, the great historian R.C. Majumdar went one step further. He suggested that the Chola navies had attacked Southeast Asian kingdoms not once but twice. The first expedition, around 1017 CE, may have been in response to a request for military assistance by the kingdom of Kambuja in modern-day Cambodia. This expedition created enough enemies to merit a second, much more comprehensive Cholan expedition around 1025 CE.

If this view be accepted, we may further presume that the first naval expedition, directed only against Kataha, was in response to the appeal of King Suryavarman of Kambuja for aid against the ruler of Kadaram (Kataha) whose aggressive expansionist policy caused anxiety to the Kambuja ruler. The hostilities, thus begun, led to the second expedition on a bigger scale which scattered the empire of Srivijaya, extending over the Malay Peninsula and Indonesia, at least for the time being.[18]

This is why, Majumdar suggests, the Tanjavur inscription mentions Kedaram twice. The first mention refers to the earlier, smaller attack, and the latter to the more comprehensive, multi-target naval expedition that wreaked havoc all over Southeast Asia.

Alternatively, other historians say that the Cholas, at the peak of their power around 1025 CE, simply wanted to make a statement.

In any case, the statement was fantastic. More recent studies suggest that a Chola prince may even have sailed to Sri Vijaya himself to suppress a revolt against Chola overlordship. He may then have sailed onwards to China as part of a trade delegation.

Even if these theories are only partly true, what they mean for our understanding of Indian history is remarkable. Over the millennia, dozens of dynasties have ruled over small and large parts of India. Often this flux of power and alliance has given rise to magnificent ruling dynasties. However, the ambitions of even the greatest of these dynasties seldom extended to lands beyond India's natural borders. Eventually, the mountains in the north and the seas everywhere else hemmed in Indian ambitions.

---

[18]R.C. Majumdar, 'The Overseas Expeditions of King Rājendra Cola', *Artibus Asiae,* Vol. 24, No. 3/4 (1961), pp. 338-42.

It is in this context that the Cholas outdid almost every other Indian dynasty or government. Their navy went far beyond any Indian expedition before or since.

Yet, even the Chola grandeur was transient. For all their administrative prowess, trading expertise and naval ambition, they were soon brought crashing to the ground by wars on the Indian mainland. Slowly, after a golden age of expansion, the Chola Empire began to contract again. Conflict between the Cholas and other local kingdoms and enemy alliances slowly began to bleed the empire. And as the frontiers collapsed inwards, they began to lose control over shipbuilding towns on the eastern Indian seaboard. The Chola navy slowly withered away.

Finally, in the thirteenth century, the Cholas were almost completely subdued by the kings of the Pandyan dynasty. Their greatest legacy was breathtaking architecture drenched with inscription, and a colonial ambition that was far, far ahead of its time and place. Yet, it was an elusive story, one that stayed hidden away for centuries in the holiest chambers of the greatest Chola temple. And it only revealed itself thanks to a German and a Frenchman discovering the past a generation apart. And, for the Sceptical Patriot, it helped to conclusively rule out one particularly popular 'India fact'.

SCEPTICAL PATRIOT INDIA FACT SCORECARD

Popular fact
India has never invaded another country in 10,000 years.

Score
2/10

Suggested fact

Indian kings beat each other up all the time. And once in a while they managed to raid lands far, far beyond your wildest imaginations.

Homework for the excessively sceptical

1. What are the latest developments in Coedes theory of the Indian influence over Southeast Asia?
2. What was the Chola navy like? What weapons did they use?
3. The Cholas also controlled the islands of the Maldives for many years. Discuss.
4. Wonder if they let in people to see that inscription in the temple in Tanjavur these days!

THREE

Everything about Nothing

One day, in March 2010, the editor of the newspaper I worked for summoned me to his room.

'What do you know about Swiss watches?' he asked me out of the corner of his mouth as he typed away on his laptop, no doubt ripping some poor reporter somewhere.

'My father used to collect some of the cheaper brands once upon a time. And I thought he was nuts for wasting his time and money on them.'

'But you've heard of Omega and Rolex and TAG Heuer and all that?'

'Yes, of course.'

'Great. You're going to Basel this year…'

A few days later, I was on a plane from Delhi to Zurich to cover Basel World, the world's largest and most important annual watch and jewellery fair. Since then, watches have become something of a personal obsession. Each year, I travel to Switzerland at least half a dozen times to attend fairs, visit factories and interview watchmakers. And, on average, I publish approximately 200 pages worth of watch editorial each year.

I have also started behaving exactly like my father. I can spend hours outside a watch store, just looking through the display window and whimpering softly. I've even accumulated something of a fledgling collection. But none of them is particularly expensive or rare, though there is one HMT automatic, an NASL-03, that I am particularly proud of.

During one of these trips to Switzerland, I once interviewed a master watchmaker who actually had his brand named after himself. This, by itself, is not all that rare in the Swiss watch business; in fact, it is the norm. Almost every watch brand, barring a few such as Rolex, is named after the original founder. The Swiss are quite proud of this, and try to flaunt the age of their brands as widely as possible. But a successful watch brand named after a watchmaker who is still alive? That is pretty rare. Most Swiss brands are named after founders who died centuries ago.

The industry tends to be full of either grim, inscrutable automatons or flamboyant showmen who lie through their teeth. This fellow, one of the greatest watchmakers alive right now, was neither. In fact, he seemed something of a romantic and an amateur philosopher. 'I love your country,' he said. 'You Indian guys are so intelligent, so smart. You discovered so many mathematical things.' For the next thirty minutes or so, he spoke about the Fibonacci series, the golden ratio and other such mathematical curiosities. In the end, he returned to the subject of India: 'But all this was made possible only because of you Indians. You guys invented the zero! Without the zero…' He threw up his arms, shrugged and exhaled loudly. Nothing, he seemed to say. Without the zero, there would be nothing.

A few days later, I spotted him having lunch in a restaurant, surrounded by a bevy of Asian women. I was still in a daze after our glorious interview, so I quickly Googled up the French Wikipedia page for the 'inventor of the zero'—Aryabhatta, of course—and handed my phone over to him. I admit I was hoping to impress him with 'Indian heritage'.

When I looked over a few minutes later, the phone was just lying on the table in front of the watchmaker; he was busy snacking on a woman's ear while she giggled appreciatively. They did not notice when I gingerly walked over and retrieved my phone, with the Aryabhatta page untouched.

India's claim to the invention of the zero is perhaps the most widely used—and abused—'India fact'. It appears on every single list of facts I have gathered in the course of my research. It is so popular that it has graduated from fact to dogma and then all the way to the butt of jokes. It is also one of those rare facts that is repeated with complete credulity in both Indian and international literature. A December 2012 news article on the *Scientific American* website about the 125th anniversary of the Indian mathematician Srinivasa Ramanujan, was subtitled: 'India, home of the number zero, ends a year-long math party in unique fashion'.[19]

Everyone, everywhere, it seems, is in broad agreement that the zero was invented in India.

Or was it? The Sceptical Patriot is not one to be fazed by national and international repetition. We must find the true story.

And what an intriguing story it proves to be.

＊⸙＊

In Gwalior, there is a fort commonly known as Gwalior Fort. Next to the fort is the small Chaturbuja temple. Inside the temple is a statue with four arms but no face. It did once have a face, but it has since been vandalized. There are two inscriptions in this temple. One is engraved over the main door. The other is inscribed into an indentation, roughly square in shape, on

---

[19]Evelyn Lamb, 'Remembering Ramanujan: India Celebrates Its Famous Mathematical Son', *Scientific American*, 22 December 2012.

the left wall of the sanctum sanctorum as you enter it, to Lord Vishnu's right.

The temple had fallen into ruin long before the first archaeologists began studying it in the late nineteenth century. The inscription over the main door lay unnoticed even after initial excavations. It was first noticed, copied down and translated into English in 1883 by our old friend and expert Indologist, Eugen Julius Theodor Hultzsch (remember him from Chapter 2?). The second one inside the sanctum sanctorum had been transcribed before, but Hultzsch copied it down again anyway.

Hultzsch seems surprised at the quality of the prose in the inscription over the door:

> The first inscription consists of 27 Sanskrit verses and must have been composed by an ingenious pandit, who was well versed in alamkara. His extravagant hyperboles will appear startling and amusing even to one accustomed to the usual kavya style.[20]

The second inscription from the tablet next to Vishnu is not so great. It is written, Hultzsch says, in 'incorrect Sanskrit prose'.

But then, history and discovery are eccentric muses. Sometimes they care not for art and aesthetics. The first inscription that impressed Hultzsch has passed into the annals without emitting even a low whimper. Nice, but meh.

The second, shoddy inscription, on the other hand, is one of the most important records in the history of mathematics. If there is any record in all of India that is fully deserving of generating and maintaining its own cannon of India facts, this is

---

[20]E. Hultsch, 'The Two Inscriptions of the Vaillabhattasvamin Temple at Gwalior', *Epigraphia Indica* I, pp. 154-61.

it. There should be entire museums complete with multimedia displays and gift shops dedicated to this inscription.

So what does this piece of inscription say? Does it reveal the name of a mysterious king? Give a concrete date for a historical episode that experts had argued over for decades? Does it tell the future, then, in some Nostradamic way?

> Bewareth thee the phone that is all touch but no buttons. For children will buyeth expensive apps…

No. It is merely an inscription informing one of a donation that has been made to this temple. It goes like this:

> Om! Adoration to Vishnu! In the year 933, on the second day of the bright half of Magha…the whole town gave to the temple of the nine Durgas…a piece of land belonging to the village of Chudapallika…270 royal hastas in length, and 187 hastas in breadth, a flower-garden, on an auspicious day…

Then, a little later, the transcription says:

> And on this same day, the town gave to these same two temples a perpetual endowment to the effect…for the requirements of worship, 50 garlands of such market flowers as available at the particular season.

There is more to this second Gwalior inscription. But these lines are the relevant bits.

So, what is so groundbreaking about these lines?

Simple. The numbers in them. Especially the two measures in hastas and the number of flower garlands. Inscribed in 876 CE, this inscription is the oldest text anywhere in India in which the zero is used in exactly the way we use it today. (The inscription itself refers to year 933 in the Saka calendar. In case you're wondering.) And not just because the zero in 270 hastas or 50 garlands looks like the modern zero—it does; it looks like a small circle. But also because it is used in the way it is, both as a placeholder for no value and a number in its own right.

There is broad agreement amongst researchers that the inscription at the Chaturbuja Temple in Gwalior is one of the earliest records anywhere of the modern zero. In February 2007, Bill Casselman, a professor at the University of British Columbia, wrote a brief essay titled 'All for Nought' for the website of the American Mathematical Society. In the essay, he talks of a journey he made to Gwalior to have a look at the inscriptions. He wrote:

> What is surprising about these numbers is that they are so similar to what modern civilization uses currently. The more you learn about how our current number symbols developed—transmitted from the Hindus to the Persians, then to Mediterranean Islam, and differently in East and West—the more remarkable this appears…
>
> What the Gwalior tablet shows is that by 876 CE our current place-value system with a base of 10 had become part of popular culture in at least one region of India.[21]

So, are we done with this chapter, then? Pats on back all around, 10/10 for this 'India fact'? Also, what is all that confusing talk of placeholders and numbers and usages?

Alas, that is the problem with the history of the zero. It is much more complicated than a little circle that stands for nothing.

And this is why establishing India's ownership of the zero will

[21]Bill Casselman, 'All for Nought', *AMS: American Mathematica Society*, from <http://www.ams.org/samplings/feature-column/fcarc-india-zero>, accessed on 30 November 2013.

take a little more sceptical enquiry, one that will take us far, far away from that little abandoned temple in Gwalior.

❋❧❋

William Ewart Gladstone was one of the greatest politicians in British history. He became prime minister not once or twice but four times. And he left the British government with a legacy of liberal thinking that continues to influence it in direct and indirect ways to this day.

Gladstone was also a Homer fanatic. He read, reread and re-reread works by the great Greek epic poet, first as a student of the classics, and then just for the pure awesome heck of it.

Then, suddenly, during yet another reading of the Greek epics, Gladstone noticed something strange. In all of Homer's work, not once was there a reference to the colour blue. Not once. Never. Despite several mentions of seas and skies and other things we would normally associate with the blue colour, Homer never actually used the word 'blue' in his work.

Gladstone came to the conclusion that this was because Homer and most other Greeks of his period were colour-blind. Their eyes simply didn't register the colour blue.

Since then, other researchers have disproved this theory and come up with many of their own. The German philosopher Lazarus Geiger took Gladstone's analysis and extended it further, across several other great epic poems and religious texts of many other religions around the world. Geiger made a stunning discovery: Blue scarcely made an appearance anywhere.

He wrote in his 1880 book *History and Development of the Human Race*:

If we consider the nature of the books to which this observation applies, the idea of chance must here be excluded. Let me first mention the wonderful, youthfully fresh hymns of the Rigveda, the discovery of which amidst the mass of Indian literature seems destined to become as important to the present century in awakening a sense of genuine antiquity as the revival of Greek antiquity at the threshold of modern times was to that period in arousing the sense of beauty and artistic taste. These hymns, consisting of more than 10,000 lines, are nearly all filled with descriptions of the sky. Scarcely any other subject is more frequently mentioned; the variety of hues which the sun and dawn daily display in it, day and night, clouds and lightning, the atmosphere and the ether, all these are with inexhaustible abundance exhibited to us again and again in all their magnificence; only the fact that the sky is blue could never have been gathered from these poems by anyone who did not already know it himself.[22]

Which is Geiger's roundabout way of saying that while the Rigveda refers to the sky several times, it never actually calls it 'blue'.

I first came across all this analysis by Gladstone and Geiger on an episode of *Radiolab*, my favourite radio show/podcast in the whole world. Produced by a New York public radio station, *Radiolab* explores one topic each episode through the medium of fascinating stories. The whole Gladstone bit came up during an episode called 'Colours'.

Now if you're wondering what all this has to do with the concept of zero…well, it doesn't have anything to do with it directly. But indirectly, I wanted to bring up the complicated notion of identity.

---

[22]Lazarus Geiger, *Contributions to the History and Development of the Human Race* (London: Trubuer & Co, 1880), p. 50.

Let us assume, for a moment, that the Greeks actually didn't have a real word for the colour blue. Does this mean that they never saw the sky or noticed its colour? Absolutely not. Unless the Greeks didn't have a sky, or had one but in purple. This seems unlikely. Awesome, but unlikely.

So did someone have to invent blue for them? Think about it. (I am trying to.) Blue was all around them all the time. They just didn't have a name for it. Or find the need to. Until one day somebody decided that the colour of the sky deserved a name. And that name would be: blue. Or whatever was the local language equivalent for blue.

But would it make any sense to call this bright individual the inventor of blue? After all, it is not like the stuff wasn't around till he/she came along and decided to call it something. It was there all along. All our inventor managed to do was to give it a name and an identity.

When we talk about the 'invention' of zero, we're faced with a similar problem. How do you invent a number?

Now, the term 'zero' itself can mean many things. But for the purposes of this enquiry, just two or three of them should suffice.

First of all, zero stands for nothing. A void. Nothingness. An absence of anything. So if 'one' represents a single instance of something, 'zero' represents no instances of that thing. But, like blue, this is not really something you would expect someone to have invented.

Mrs Cavemen: How many mastodon kebabs did I cook?
Mr Caveman: Three?
Mrs Cavemen: How many did you eat?
Mr Caveman: Three?
Mrs Caveman: How many do I have left for myself now, you greedy pig?

Mr Caveman: I cannot answer that question because I am yet
to develop a sense of nothingness or a term for this sense.
Mrs Cavemen: Damn! Every single time...

And even if someone did invent the idea of nothingness and a
term for it, it seems ludicrous to try to fix a time or place for it.
Also, chances are that this sense of 'nothing' developed in many
places simultaneously.

So let's skip that definition of zero.

There are two more.

One of the best, most concise histories of the zero I've read
anywhere is an online essay titled, would you believe it, 'A History
of Zero', written by two professors of mathematics at the
University of St Andrews.

Professors J.J. O'Connor and E.F. Robertson write about the
other two uses of zero:

> One use is as an empty place indicator in our place-value
> number system. Hence in a number like 2106 the zero is
> used so that the positions of the 2 and 1 are correct. Clearly
> 216 means something quite different. The second use of
> zero is as a number itself in the form we use it as 0. There are
> also different aspects of zero within these two uses, namely
> the concept, the notation, and the name.[23]

To me, both of these ideas are somewhat less abstract than the
notion of nothing. And therefore, in a sense, more 'inventable'.

Alas, in the very next paragraph the good professors write:
'Neither of the above uses has an easily described history.'

Ugh.

[23]J.J. O'Connor and E.F. Robertson, 'A History of Zero', *MacTutor
History of Mathematics*, November 2000, from <http://www-history.mcs.
st-and.ac.uk/PrintHT/Zero.html>, accessed on 30 November 2013.

So let us start, then, at one of the earliest systems of writing in the world: the Babylonian cuneiform. Did they have a sophisticated understanding of mathematics? And if so, how and when did they start representing zeroes in their texts?

By 3000 BCE, more or less around the time the Indus Valley civilization was establishing itself, the Babylonians had developed a system of positional numbering very similar to the number system we use today. This means that they wrote long numbers with digits in the 'one's place', then 'ten's place', and so on. Except that while we use a base-10 system, the Babylonians used base-60. We have 10 digits in our number system, the Babylonians had 60. (Well 59 actually. They didn't have a zero for a long time.)

The easiest way to explain the difference between base-10 and base-60 without making you want to throw this book against a wall/spouse in frustration is to ask you to look at your clock or watch. Credit the Babylonians and history's propensity for memory, but to this day we still measure time on a base-60 system like the Babylonians. So, if I told you to add 1 hour and 34 minutes to 2 hours and 40 minutes, you'd effortlessly carry out a base-60 addition and tell me 4 hours and 14 minutes.

So how did the Babylonians indicate numbers like, say, 602? In the beginning, they did this by just leaving an empty space between the symbols for 2 and 600 to indicate that there was nothing in the 'ten's place'. After hundreds of years of doing this, sometime around 700 BCE (but perhaps earlier), the Babylonians started indicating these empty spaces with a special symbol to indicate positions with no numbers.

OH MY GOD, THE BABYLONIANS INVENTED THE ZERO BEFORE INDIA!

No! No! No! [Slap across the face.] Calm down.

This symbol—often two wedges but sometimes one or

three—only indicated a zero as far as the first of the definitions that Professors O'Connor and Robertson outlined above: as an empty place indicator. The Babylonians still didn't think of the zero as a digit by itself.

In fact, if you were to go back in time and ask a Babylonian to multiply the 'wedge symbol by 10', he'd probably laugh at your ignorance and then behead you just to be safe.

The wedge symbol was something of a half-zero. But not a zero in the modern sense.

Now, one popular embellishment of the 'India invented zero' fact is that without the zero it would have been impossible for mankind to accomplish complicated mathematics. One version even says: 'If Indians had not invented the zero, man would have never walked on the moon.'

Cough.

So did that mean that Babylonian mathematicians fumbled about like little children, crippled with zero-lessness, cursed to spend their whole lives adding and subtracting and struggling to make a career out of it?

Not at all. The Babylonians, it turns out, were kickass at math. (Just like everybody in your class, right? I know the pain.)

They could do all kinds of cool things with fractions and binomial equations and even quadratic equations. But nothing, perhaps, indicates their mathematical ability more than a small round tablet that is part of Yale University's Babylonian Collection. Around eight centimetres in diameter, the tablet is commonly referred to as object number YBC 7289, and has a calculation inscribed into it in the Babylonian cuneiform script.

According to this tablet, dated between 1800 and 1600 BCE, the Babylonians calculated the square root of 2 as 1.41421296. I just punched in square root of 2 on my laptop's calculator and I got 1.41421356. Almost 4,000 years ago, the Babylonians could calculate the square root of 2 to within five decimal places of modern computers! The accuracy would remain unmatched for thousands of years. So they got along quite swimmingly without the modern notion of zero.

Over time, the Babylonian tendency to use a symbol to denote an empty placeholder would spread east and westwards. The Greeks, great mathematicians themselves, perhaps took one small step for zero-kind: Some records suggest that they used a circular symbol as a placeholder. However, we are still centuries away from zero being used as an actual number.

O'Connor and Robertson write:

> The scene now moves to India where it is fair to say the numerals and number system was born which have evolved into the highly sophisticated ones we use today. Of course that is not to say that the Indian system did not owe something to earlier systems and many historians of mathematics believe that the Indian use of zero evolved from its use by Greek astronomers. As well as some historians who seem to want to play down the contribution of the Indians in a most unreasonable way, there are also those who make claims about the Indian invention of zero which seem to go far too far.

These are the biases and tendencies that make nailing down 'India facts' such as this one so difficult. So many commentators are driven not by a need to reveal the truth but to drive home a point. Swirl in some patriotism, racism or cultural chauvinism—and you have the perfect environment that breeds unsubstantiated cultural legend.

> Indian: India invented the zero! And you know what Gandhi said when they asked him about Western civilization?

Non-Indian: Blah blah. You guys didn't invent anything.
And you killed Gandhi…
Indian: HOW DARE YOU!!!

Etcetera, etcetera.

Thankfully, amongst all this biased nonsense, there are always
a few historians going about their job in a comparatively honest
and 'truthful' way. (I say 'comparative' because no one is ever
truly bias-free.)

And, at this point, we shall stop pontificating and leap onto
their robust shoulders for the rest of this enquiry.

Perhaps the first celebrity mathematician in Indian history was
Aryabhatta. Nobody really knows where he was born. Suggestions
for his birthplace range from Kodungallur in Kerala to Dhaka
in Bangladesh. In fact, much of what we know about the life of
Aryabhatta has been pieced together over the last century and
a half, like a messy jigsaw puzzle. For centuries, it was believed
that there were two Aryabhattas. This was only sorted out as
recently as the 1920s. There is greater agreement about the fact
that he spent at least some of his time as a mathematician and
astronomer working in or around modern-day Patna, then
called Kusumapura. And it is in Kusumapura that Aryabhatta is
believed to have written his most famous work: the mathematical
and astronomical handbook *Aryabhatiya*.

Several translations of the *Aryabhatiya* were prepared in the
early years of the twentieth century. One popular translation,
published by Walter Eugene Clark, a professor of Sanskrit at
Harvard, opens with an engrossing monologue. The monologue
starts as follows:

In 1874 Kern published at Leiden a text called the *Aryabhatiya*
which claims to be the work of Aryabhata, and which gives…
the date of the birth of the author as 476 CE. If these claims

can be substantiated, and if the whole work is genuine, the text is the earliest preserved Indian mathematical and astronomical text bearing the name of an individual author, the earliest Indian text to deal specifically with mathematics, and the earliest preserved astronomical text from the third or scientific period of Indian astronomy.[24]

Clark does sound a tiny bit sceptical, doesn't he? That is only because this was a period when forgeries of ancient manuscripts were rampant. Not because the forgers wanted to rewrite history but because they wanted to make money.

Of course, there is little doubt now that the *Aryabhatiya* was an authentic work that was widely quoted and criticized through the ages, perhaps even in Aryabhatta's own lifetime. Today the work is lionized and put up on a pedestal; but other ancient Indian scholars seem to have treated it with much less veneration. Indeed, one great source of verification for the *Arybhatiya's* authenticity and age is widespread reference to it in other treatises and writings.

Aryabhatta appears to have been something of a prodigy. In verse 10 of the third section—a section titled 'Kalakriya', the reckoning of time—he writes:

> When three yugappdas and sixty times sixty years had elapsed (from the beginning of the yuga) then twenty-three years of my life had passed.[25]

Twenty-three seems to be a young age, in any era, for a work of this historical importance. In fact, it seems a pity that the *Aryabhatiya* isn't more widely read, not so much for its didactic

---

[24] *The Aryabhatiya of Aryabhata*, translated by Walter Eugene Clark (Illinois: The University of Chicago Press, 1930), pp. v-xvii.

[25] *Ibid.*, p. 54.

value but for the sake of curiosity and enjoyment. It is a remarkably short work. Clark's extremely accessible translation is around eighty-two pages long, and anyone with a decent school education in mathematics should be able to make most of their way through it.

According to the Internet, the *Aryabhatiya* has been credited with everything from modern mathematics to commerce, business and even quantum mechanics. Which may be over-chickening the biryani a little bit, as my grandmother used to say.

The *Aryabhatiya* is, however, at least partly responsible for the global use of the base-10 system. Developed to a certain fullness in India, the system was later taken by the Arabs, along with Indian numerals, and propagated throughout the world. One of the *Aryabhatiya's* most frequently quoted verse is the second verse from the 'Ganitapada', or mathematics, section. Clark translates it thus:

> The numbers eka [one], dasa [ten], sata [hundred], sahasra [thousand], ayuta [ten thousand], niyuta [hundred thousand], prayuta [million], koti [ten million], arbuda [hundred million], and vrnda [thousand million] are from place to place each ten times the preceding.[26]

Boom. The decimal system outlined in a single verse. Five hundred years later, the great Persian mathematician and polymath Abu Rayhan Al Biruni would repeat the content of this verse almost word for word in his *Indica*, a compendium of Indian religion and philosophy.

But does the *Aryabhatiya* refer to a zero? At all?

Kind of. Like the Babylonians, Aryabhatta also suggests using a placeholder, called kha, whenever there is no digit in a certain

[26] *Ibid.*, p. 21.

place in a number. So Aryabhatta would write 2,106 as two-one-kha-six. But he still didn't use kha as a number itself.

Early researchers tended to call the kha Aryabhatta's version of the zero numeral. But this view seems to have changed since then. Instead, credit for pushing the idea of zero even further than Aryabhatta is given to another ancient Indian mathematician, Brahmagupta, who lived around a century later.

Around 630 CE, Brahmagupta wrote the *Brahma-Sphuta-Siddhanta*. One thing is immediately clear from this book: something had changed drastically in the way ancient Indian mathematicians dealt with the zero. It had gone from simply being a place-value holder or a null-value indicator in Aryabhatta's time, to becoming a proper numeral in its own right.

Almost.

Brahmagupta writes:

> The sum of zero and a negative number is negative, the sum of a positive number and zero is positive, the sum of zero and zero is zero.[27]

Also:

> A negative number subtracted from zero is positive, a positive number subtracted from zero is negative, zero subtracted from a negative number is negative, zero subtracted from a positive number is positive, zero subtracted from zero is zero.[28]

[27]J.J. O'Connor and E.F. Robertson, 'A History of Zero', *MacTutor History of Mathematics*, November 2000, from <http://www-history.mcs.st-and.ac.uk/PrintHT/Zero.html>, accessed on 30 November 2013.

[28]*Algebra, with Arithmetic and Mensuration from the Sanscrit of Brahmagupta and Bhascara*, translated by Henry Thomas Colebrooke (London: John Murray, 1817), p. 339.

So far so good. But then he begins to waver.

> A positive or negative number when divided by zero is a
> fraction with the zero as denominator. Zero divided by a
> negative or positive number is either zero or is expressed as
> a fraction with zero as numerator and the finite quantity as
> denominator. Zero divided by zero is zero.

This makes little sense. But Brahmagupta's leap of thinking,
which has him operating with the zero as a numeral, and not
just an indicator of nothing or a placeholder, is phenomenal. As
Connor and Robertson write: '...it is a brilliant attempt from
the first person that we know who tried to extend arithmetic to
negative numbers and zero.'

Given that Brahmagupta had already started thinking in
these terms, the Gwalior inscription can be seen as the sign of a
society at large slowly adopting cutting-edge mathematical ideas.
Three centuries after Aryabhatta, and two after Brahmagupta,
badly written temple donation inscriptions were using the zero
not just as a null placeholder but exactly as we would use it
today.

Now, if we put all these pieces together, a fairly unambiguous
narrative begins to emerge.

India was certainly not unique in using a rudimentary form
of the zero as a placeholder or as an indicator of null-value.
Aryabhatta certainly did outline the decimal system in his work,
and incorporated a kha into the decimal system. But he still
didn't really think of it as a numeral by itself. This had changed
by the time of Brahmagupta, who was doing all kinds of nifty
business with a zero. And then there is the Gwalior business.
Surely India can then stake a claim for outstanding innovation
in, if not invention of, applied and theoretical zero sciences?

Except for one more inscription. (I swear, no more in this

chapter.) And here we need to bring back another one of our old friends: George Coedes of Sri Vijaya fame.

Right up until 1931, the Gwalior inscription wasn't just the oldest instance of a zero numeral used in the modern sense in India, but in the whole world. In that year, Coedes published a paper in which he talked about an inscription in a ruined temple in Sambor in Cambodia. The inscribed tablet, that Coedes called K-127, said this in Old Khmer: 'Chaka parigraha 605 pankami roc…' which stands for: 'The Chaka era has reached 605 on the fifth day of the waning moon…' And it used a dot for the zero.

The date of this inscription? 683 CE.

Sure, it is not a little circular loop. But there is now widespread agreement that this is perhaps the oldest existing zero anywhere in the world, predating the Gwalior inscription by around two centuries.

So close. So close. If Gwalior had maintained its primacy, this chapter could have ended on a slightly more satisfying note.

Still, it is pleasing to know that this 'India fact' is not without substance. It is, in fact, quite agreeably watertight if one is willing to loosen the definitions of 'invention' just a little bit. Also who is to say that the Cambodians didn't get their idea of the zero numeral from India? Entirely possible, given the huge sphere influence Indian culture, religion and scholarship had in Southeast Asia around the time K-127 was carved.

But I also think that the story of the zero shows how invention in the ancient world was hardly a matter of eureka moments or light bulbs going off. Those guys sat and thought about things for a long time. They shared their ideas widely. They published widely. They criticized each other. It was as if they cared for the knowledge itself, and not the credit associated with discovering things.

How bizarre.

SCEPTICAL PATRIOT INDIA FACT SCORECARD

Popular fact
The zero was invented in India.

Score
7.5/10

Suggested fact
Indian thinkers were quite possibly the first to take the zero from being a mere placeholder to a number in its own regard. And then they did mathematics with it. India also perhaps had the first societies in the world to embrace the zero in daily life.

Homework for the excessively sceptical
1. What is the story of that Cambodian tablet? It is well worth exploring.
2. Surely this a good opportunity to the visit the Chaturbhuja temple in Gwalior?
3. How did Indian mathematics percolate westwards? What role did the Arabs play?
4. Why does nobody read any of the translations of these great ancient Indian texts? Pity, really.

FOUR

The Wealth of Nations

On 13 February 1739, two huge armies faced each other by the banks of the Yamuna near modern-day Karnal, some 100 kilometres away from Delhi. On one side was the army of the Mughal emperor Muhammad Shah; across the river waited an invading force led by the Persian king, and one of the greatest military minds of all time, Nadir Shah.

When Muhammad Shah, born Roshan Akhtar, was elevated to the Mughal throne in 1719 at the age of seventeen, he seemed destined to live a glamorous but very short, and ultimately, painful life. In the twelve years since Emperor Aurangzeb's death in 1707, the Mughal throne had already seen seven occupants. Just in 1719, the year of Muhammad Shah's elevation, the empire had enjoyed the services of four emperors. To put it in modern corporate terms, the Mughals were suffering from a severe bout of leadership transition mismanagement.

Unfortunately for them, it was a crisis they would never really recover from.

Rarely in human history has a vast, sophisticated empire tumbled from greatness so rapidly. In 2013, the British Library held a landmark exhibition of Mughal manuscripts, paintings, journals and maps. As visitors entered the exhibition space, they were presented with an audio-visual display that gave a very brief overview of the rise and fall of the Mughal Empire.

It consisted of an LCD projector pointed at an outline map of the subcontinent. Emperor by emperor, starting with Babur, the projector beamed a red blob—the extent of the Mughal empire—onto the outline. In the beginning, the blob grows in great bursts of conquest, reaching the apex of its convulsions during the reign of Aurangzeb, when nearly the complete region is covered in red. And then the blob collapses on itself like a burst balloon. Within a few decades, the Mughals effectively have control over nothing but a pinprick of red, centred on Delhi. But even that is an exaggeration. At the library, a voiceover explained that by the early nineteenth century, the Mughal Empire had been reduced to the area within the walls of the Red Fort in Delhi. The collapsing blob was a dramatic depiction of the powerlessness of the later Mughals, and their precipitous fall.

Aurangzeb, of course, was the inflexion point.

Aurangzeb was both a great administrator and a ruthless expansionist. Which, on the face of it, seems like a good thing for the Mughal Empire. Under him, the empire and its system of revenue collection became a cash-generating machine. All of which made the empire and its emperor one of the richest in the world. In 1886, one British historian estimated that at his peak Aurangzeb was pulling in net tax revenues of £80 million.[29] Depending on how you measure the value of money over time, this could be worth as much as £50 billion in today's money.

Unfortunately, Aurangzeb was also a religious nut-job and a divisive jerk who pissed off nearly everybody in the empire by the time he died in 1707. Centuries later, his policy of ruthlessly destroying temples and taxing non-Muslims continues to be a sore point amongst many Hindus. (Not that Aurangzeb was

---

[29]Sir William Wilson Hunter, *The Indian Empire: Its People, History, and Product*s (London: Trübner & Co, 1886), p. 299.

singular in his oppression of the infidels; a book titled *A History of India in 100 Desecrations of Places of Worship* is entirely feasible. However, I would only recommend this to writers with families, homes and possessions all made of non-combustible materials. But even for such a turbulent history, Aurangzeb's brutality seems a cut apart.)

History is replete with rulers who maintained stability at the cost of justice, humanity and morality. Everyone from Adolf Hitler to Saddam Hussein to Muammar Gaddafi managed productive economies, sophisticated bureaucracies and large populations whilst simultaneously generating simmering dissent. And when these leaders leave the stage, their nations are plunged into chaos. Aurangzeb's exit was no different. Everything began to fall apart.

A battle for succession meant that the line of command broke down. The empire began to disintegrate, with oppressed peoples, governors, warlords and local satraps all throwing off the burden of Aurangzeb's brutality and shoring up their own power bases.

By the time Muhammad Shah came to the throne, thereby ending a chain of short-lived emperors, Mughal military strength had been severely depleted. Shah's reign brought stability. But he was no Aurangzeb. Muhammad Shah was called 'Sada Rangila'— the one who is always joyous. His great passions were art and culture. He was not entirely averse to taking arms, but usually this was only in response to extreme provocation, and even then he preferred to react with little to no haste. Somehow, he always seemed to be able to summon an army at the last possible moment and repulse attacks. The Marathas, in particular, were a constant thorn in his side.

But Muhammad Shah's greatest source of trepidation was the Nizam-ul-Mulk, the governor of the Deccan region and his most powerful vassal. The emperor seems to have lived in constant dread of the Nizam allying with the Marathas and marching on Delhi. Already beset by internal insecurities and a crumbling empire, and surrounded by the smouldering embers of Aurangzeb's fires of zeal, Muhammad Shah was in no position whatsoever to take on Nadir Shah, one of the great military campaigners of his age.

But the Battle of Karnal, as the events of that day in February are known to posterity, was much more than a face-off between the invading forces of a master tactician and the armies of a wretched emperor. It was also an event whose outcomes would ultimately determine the history of the whole world.

Nadir Shah was what Indian engineering college students might call 'a stud'. For the most part. So, while researching this chapter, I was surprised that he'd had such a low profile throughout my school history curriculum.

Actually…who knows? Maybe Nadir Shah featured prominently in my textbooks. Unfortunately most of my schooling in ancient, medieval and modern history involved committing things to memory.

1. What were the salient features of the Roman Empire?
2. What socio-economic conditions in Europe led to the development of the Paris Commune? Explain in approximately 700 words.
3. What is the point of all this nonsense when all of you will become engineers or doctors anyway?

This unique approach to Indian history education meant that most of us graduated from school with the entirety of Indian history congealed in our memories as an amorphous porridge-like mass with large lumps of semi-truths. Mahatma Gandhi and the freedom struggle was one lump. Akbar and the Mughals another lump. Ashoka and pre-Mughal history was one. And the Indus Valley Civilization was the last.

Within fifteen minutes of walking out of a history exam, most of this lumpy, vague history knowledge was immediately jettisoned. And with each passing day, we began to forget detail after detail, lump after lump, until these memories of famous people doing famous things at crucial moments entirely faded away or were thoroughly written over with new information on C++ programming and iron-carbon diagrams and management information systems and…

Until, that is, an Irani materials testing engineer once took me to out to lunch and brought it all gushing back.

Wait. That last line came out all wrong.

What I meant was, he took me out to lunch…and we began talking about Nadir Shah.

The conversation took place sometime in the summer of 1999. That summer, I spent two weeks at a materials testing laboratory near Dubai Port. My job was to hang around the lab, help out the staff, learn to use the machines, not poison or stab myself with anything, generally make myself useful and hopefully earn a certificate that would satisfy the mandatory training requirements at my engineering college back in Trichy.

I've never ever worked in an establishment with a higher per capita concentration of eccentricity. The lab had a total staff strength of five people. There was a secretary cum general dogsbody who left on some sort of vacation on my very first day at work. She was the junior-most member of the staff. Next up the chain came a pair of brothers from Tamil Nadu. They were twins in all but uterus concurrency. They were both short, rotund men with shiny bald heads, sun-burnt skin and permanent grins. The younger brother did all the heavy-lifting, while the elder fellow wore a tie, bossed him around, handled all the client calls and generally managed the business. Then came our Irani friend and finally, right on top, a jolly Polish man with a PhD in materials testing who was drunk every single minute I ever saw him in office those two weeks. Which was approximately ten minutes.

The whole set up was like *Fawlty Towers*, but with liquid nitrogen, welding equipment and metal-cutting saws.

Nobody exactly knew what the Irani guy was supposed to do. The Tamil Twins usually did all the testing and report writing and billing, while he spent all day planning the weekend or booking a hotel or some such. I don't think he did anything remotely related to revenue generation the whole time. Yet, he somehow seemed to be paid a very handsome salary. He drove a massive SUV, lived in a posh neighbourhood and wore high-quality clothing one size too small for him. The Tamil Twins seemed slightly miffed at the Irani's plush lifestyle. But otherwise they all seemed to get along.

A few days into my training programme, my Irani friend announced that he would take me out to a traditional Irani lunch. Immediately, one of the Tamil Twins called me aside and whispered: 'Under no circumstance should you tell him you are from Kerala. He hates Malayalis.'

I grinned. Surely this was one of their practical jokes. Tamil Twin looked grim. 'No really. Never mention you are a Malayali. He really, *really* hates Malayalis.'

Lunch was exquisite. I've long forgotten the Irani's name, but I do remember my main course and our conversation about Nadir Shah. It—lunch, not Nadir Shah—involved a wonderfully tender leg and thigh of chicken covered with a mound of rice cooked with saffron and those Irani barberries. It remains one of the best working lunches I've ever had. If only the Iranians would focus more on pulao and less on plutonium, the world would be a much, much better place. (Of course, as of a few weeks ago, they seem to have taken my words to heart. Yay.)

Halfway through lunch, Malayali-hater asked me if I knew of the historical bonds between Iran and India. I asked him to elaborate. One thing led to another led to Nadir Shah. 'He conquered India, you know,' my friend said. 'He defeated the Mughals. And then he came back to Iran. Otherwise…who knows…we may both have been speaking Farsi.'

Shut up and order more pulao, man!

Anyway. For two weeks, the lab gang shared lunches and doughnuts and teas and coffees and even the occasional beer. Throughout, I kept my Malayali roots a secret. On the very last day, as we sat down to lunch in one of the office rooms, one of the Tamil Twins asked the Irani man if I'd taken him for lunch to a traditional Kerala restaurant. His eyebrows leapt clear off his forehead.

'Why would he do that?'

'Because you fed him your ethnic food. Now he should return the favour, no?'

No further inputs were forthcoming from Malayali-hater for the rest of the day. Only frosty silence.

I still have no idea why he hates Malayalis. But having spent many years with other Malayalis, I can understand the sentiment.

Since that unforgettable lunch fifteen years ago, Nadir Shah has popped up ever so often in my life. He has featured in books, 'India quizzes' and, more recently, in the course of researching this book—in papers analyzing the history and structure of the Mughal economy.

But first we need to deal with the small matter of the Battle of Karnal and its terrible aftermath.

There is some disagreement, to this day, about how many

combatants actually engaged in the battle. What complicates the numbers is the fact that in addition to the 'official' ranks of soldiers, both camps had thousands of servants, stragglers and camp followers who may have followed their masters into battle. One account written shortly after the battle claims that some of Nadir Shah's support staff were armed well enough to be a force on the field of battle.

Add to this uncertainty the tendency of both winners and losers of battles to inflate the opposite camp's strength, and you are left with a numerical conundrum that is impossible to solve. A reasonable estimate is that anywhere from 1,50,000 to 2,00,000 soldiers took to the battlefields of Karnal on that day. The Mughals appear to have arrayed a much larger force than the Persians—some estimates place the Mughal forces to be twice as large.

Nadir Shah, no doubt, was a great captain of war. In just a decade and a half, he had gone from being a minor warlord and tribal leader to the emperor of Iran and the father of a new dynasty—the Afsharids. He had waged and won wars against a whole host of large and small belligerents across entire Safavid Iran. And while he wasn't a particularly brutal conqueror, at least to start with, Nadir Shah did not flinch at heavily taxing his people in order to finance his armies. In 1732, after placing a puppet emperor on the throne of Persia, Nader Shah announced that as commander of the army he would soon 'throw reins around the necks of the rulers of Kandahar, Bokhara, Delhi and Istanbul'.[30] It wasn't all bluster. Nadir Shah soon marched eastwards.

But for all his military might, the Battle of Karnal was still Muhammad Shah's for the losing. As I said before, the Mughals

[30]Michael Axworthy, *Iran: Empire of the Mind: A History from Zoroaster to the Present Day* (London: Penguin, 2008), p. 156.

had the larger army. Also Karnal was much, much closer to Delhi than it was to Isfahan or Khorasan, the great Persian centers. Nadir Shah was far away from home, and taking on an empire that was much larger and wealthier than his own. Fortunately for the Persians, they were taking on a Mughal Empire that teetered on the brink.

The Battle of Karnal was a rout. Muhammad Shah's forces were thoroughly beaten. One eyewitness account[31] says that the retreating Mughal soldiers promptly began to loot their own camps as they ran away.

The catastrophe at Karnal was the nudge that finally sent the Mughal Empire tumbling off the edge.

Nadir Shah then marched into Delhi and began to systematically suck the Mughal coffers dry. Which, as far as Nadir Shah was concerned, was his standard modus operandi.

But then something happened. Nadir Shah snapped.

One version of the event goes like this.

In early March 1739, almost a month after the battle, a riot broke out in the Paharganj area of Delhi over the high price of corn. Soon rumours began to spread that Nadir Shah had been poisoned, and mobs began attacking Persians all over the city. The next morning, a perturbed Nadir Shah rode to Chandni Chowk, hoping to quell the unrest with his presence. This only helped to energize the mobs. Eventually, somewhere near the Sunehri Masjid in the centre of Chandi Chowk, someone shot a musket at the Shah that missed him but killed an officer who stood nearby.

A contemporary observer writes:

> This made him give way to his passion, and order a general slaughter to be commenced from that very place; soldiers

[31] James Fraser, *The History of Nadir Shah* (London: W. Strahan, 1742), p. 159.

in an instant getting upon the walls and terraces, began to plunder and kill.[32]

The brutality that followed is unsurpassed in Indian history. For about seven hours the Persians went berserk all over Delhi. The same contemporary observer wrote that between 1,30,000 and 1,50,000 men, women and children were slaughtered. Modern historians such as Michael Axworthy estimate the death toll at closer to 30,000.

Nadir Shah, meanwhile, had changed forever. Axworthy writes:

> Prior to this point, Nader had generally (at least away from the battlefield) achieved his ends without excessive bloodshed. But after Delhi, he may have decided that his previous scruples had become redundant.[33]

After this, Nadir Shah got down to what had always been his plan for the Indian expedition: bleed the Mughal Empire dry and make enough money to finance his wars back home. After the rape of Delhi, the emperor resumed the process of extraction.

On 16 May 1739, Nadir Shah marched out of Delhi at the head of a logistics operation comprising 30,000 camels and 24,000 mules, all laden with treasure. There is really little point in trying to estimate the exact value of all this eye-watering booty. How do you even sit in 2013 and estimate the worth of bales of Mughal textile made in the eighteenth century? The consensus is that the Persians went back with seventy crore

---

[32]Mirza Zuman, *A Journal of Nadir Shah's Transaction in India*, translated by James Fraser (London: W. Strahan, 1742). Included in Fraser's *The History of Nadir Shah*.

[33]Michael Axworthy, *Iran: Empire of the Mind: A History from Zoroaster to the Present Day* (London: Penguin, 2008), p. 159.

rupees worth of plunder in 1739 money. Axworthy suggests that this is equivalent to almost £90 billion today.[34]

Nadir Shah, it is said, was so pleased with his acquisitions that he announced a three-year moratorium on all taxes in Persia. The Peacock Throne, Kohinoor diamond and Daryanoor diamond were all taken away. Jewels were transported by the bagful. Some of this plunder can still be seen to this day, as part of the Iranian Crown Jewels display at the Treasury of National Jewels in Tehran.

From the perspective of the Sceptical Patriot, the Battle of Karnal has two important legacies.

The first is that it forms part of the context for that famous question: What if India had never been colonized?

(Extreme 'what-if' alert!)

What if Nadir Shah had never invaded? Or had been repulsed at Karnal? What if Muhammad Shah and his forces had prevailed? This could have left them, and subsequent Mughal emperors, in a much stronger position to counter British colonial machinations. Also, what if victory over Nadir Shah had proved to be just the dose of triumphant enthusiasm that rallied the Mughal establishment and given it fresh energy and enthusiasm? Not to forget that the vanquisher of Nadir Shah would have cowered his rebelling vassals into respectful peace.

On the other hand, what if Nadir Shah had decided to stay and never leave? What if he had extended the iron grip of the Afsharid Empire to the banks of Ganga or beyond? Surely the fledgling British and other assorted European colonials would have been thulped at the first sign of territorial ambitions?

Who knows?

The second legacy of the Persian plunder is much more interesting and populated with far fewer what-ifs. It also brings us to the next great 'India fact'.

[34] *Ibid.*

The fact that the Persians could plunder such astonishing sums of money in the course of a few months—and without bothering to venture out of Delhi at all—can only mean that the Mughal Empire must have been astoundingly wealthy. Not to forget that shortly after the Persians left, much of Mughal India went back to business as usual. An astonishing £90 billion, in today's money, was written off without so much as a fiscal burp. Thus nicely preparing the Indian peoples for the future invention of Air India.

Surely all this only lends added anecdotal weight to that great 'India fact': Before the British came to India, we were the richest country on earth.

Really?

The wealth of nations, or lack thereof, is a very, very complicated thing. What does one mean by a rich country?

A country with a large economy? This would automatically rule out places like Monte Carlo or San Marino, which are full of spectacularly rich and beautiful people but have economies that are smaller than decent-sized Gurgaon shopping malls.

Maybe a rich country is one with a lot of rich people. This would automatically make China and India amongst the richest countries in the world—both nations have dozens upon dozens of millionaire entrepreneurs, professionals, land owners, politicians, civil servants and panchayat members. But clearly, in any palpable, obvious sense, both of these nations aren't rich. Millions of people in both countries live without access to food, water, shelter, education or the latest Apple products.

Perhaps, then, the richness of a country should be measured not by how big its economy is but by how widely this economy is distributed. Or something.

It is a conundrum that some of the world's finest economists continue to struggle with to this day. And it is one that is utterly germane to really getting under the skin of this 'India fact'.

Still, of all the 'India facts' out there, this is the one that is best supported by evidence. A year—or maybe two—ago I generally wondered out loud on Twitter about this. Was India really the richest country in the world once? Or was this one more myth we tell ourselves to better cope with our tenuous economic and social realities?

Almost all the people who wrote back to me with proof or data pointed me to the work of one particular gentleman: Angus Maddison.

Maddison, who died in 2010, was one of the greatest practitioners of macroeconomic history. In other words, he was an expert at figuring out the size and shape of national economies dating back centuries. And one of Maddison's most popular and most quoted research works is his estimate of the size of India's economy over the centuries, and his analysis of how this transformed before and during the colonial period.

References to this 'India fact'—books, blogs, emails and the Wikipedia entry for 'Economic History of India'—all feature variations of the assertion that India was the largest economy in the world shortly before the British established colonial overlordship. And almost all of them—at least the ones that bother to point to source material—refer to Maddison's landmark 2001 publication, *The World Economy: A Millennial Perspective*.

The entire gist of Maddison's thesis is captured in a series of tables that appears throughout several of his works. The one that many Indians seem to enjoy the most is titled: 'Share of World GDP: 20 Countries and Regional Totals, 1-2003 CE'.[35]

No prizes whatsoever for guessing why this table is popular

[35] *Maddison Project*, from <http://www.ggdc.net/maddison/maddison-project/home.htm>, accessed on 4 February 2014.

amongst practitioners of the 'India fact'. In a single row of numbers, this table seems to capture the entirety of India's historic experience with government.

At the dawn of the Christian Era, 1 CE, Maddison estimates India to account for the largest chunk of the world's GDP: 32 per cent. By the year 1700, on the threshold of colonial subjugation, India's share has withered a little but is still on top with 24.4 per cent of world GDP. China is a close second, with a 22.3 per cent share.

And then it falls. And falls. And falls. By 1820, India's share is down to 16 per cent. By 1913, it is 7.5 per cent. A few years after freedom, in 1950, India's share of the world's GDP has shrivelled to a measly 4.2 per cent—about the same as France but with countless times the population. India has become a poor country.

The narrative is seductively simple. Here is a people that was far ahead of every other people on earth two millennia ago. Here is an economic powerhouse with sophisticated cultures, cities and societies when the rest of the world was just rubbing sticks together. Over the next 1700 years or so, everyone else plays catch up whilst this nation is ravaged by the comings and goings of a thousand invaders. Yet, it maintains its position of supremacy. And then these white people come in their fancy boats with their fancy guns and their foreign ways and their naked greed…and screw it all up. Two centuries later, they have chewed India dry and spat it out empty.

What we see today then is not an emerging India but a re-emerging one. A nation slowly reclaiming its rightful place at the top of the world's economic pyramid.

The point is—oh, that stupid Sceptical Patriot in me—two things about this fantastic narrative bother me. One: How do you even measure the GDP of India in 1 CE or 1700 CE? Given that the Government of India can't even measure last month's GDP accurately?

And, more importantly, what does GDP or GDP share really mean?

※ⅾ⅔※

At first glance, the idea of measuring a nation's Gross Domestic Product makes perfect sense. It seems like a nation's equivalent of an individual's blood pressure or body weight—a single data point that tells you how well you're doing and warns you of any current or impending problems. One would assume that national GDP measurements have been around since the earliest nations themselves.

One would be very wrong indeed.

The idea of a nation's Gross Domestic Product, in the way we talk about it today, is only eighty years old. It was an idea born out of the US government's struggle to manage the Great Depression.

'Year in, year out the people of this country, assisted by the stock of goods in their possession, render a vast volume of work toward the satisfaction of their wants.' Thus begins one of the most important documents in macroeconomics. Titled *National Income, 1929-32*, it was a report prepared by Simon Kuznets, a staff member at the National Bureau of Economic Research in New York, and published in 1934. In it, Kuznets outlined a method whereby the US government could begin to accurately measure the size of its national accounts. Kuznets explained, briefly and utterly satisfyingly, how to do this in the very first paragraph:

If all commodities produced and all personal services rendered during the year are added at their market value, and from the resulting total we subtract the value of that part of the nation's stock of goods which was expended (both as raw materials and as capital equipment) in producing this total, then the remainder constitutes the net product of the national economy during the year. It is referred to as national income produced, and may be defined briefly as that part of the economy's end-product which is attributable to the efforts of the individuals who comprise a nation.[36]

The art and science of measuring national accounts and gross domestic product was born. In the report, Kuznets went on to outline his method for breaking down national accounts into several sections and sub-sections, thereby enabling the government to study and understand how the economy as a whole and its various components were performing. At the time Kuznets was thirty-three years old. He would then go on to dedicate his entire life to the pursuit of measuring national accounts as accurately as possible. In 1971, Kuznets was awarded the Nobel Prize for Economics. He won the honour 'for his empirically founded interpretation of economic growth which has led to new and deepened insight into the economic and social structure and process of development'.[37]

In the last eighty years, the concept of a nation's GDP has taken on totemic proportions. Newsrooms erupt in excitement every time a government releases GDP data. Slight shifts in the second decimal place of GDP growth rates are enough to send stock and bond markets swooping and soaring. News

[36]Simon Kuznets, *National Income, 1929-32* (New York: National Bureau of Economic Research, 1934), p. 1.

[37]'The Sveriges Riksbank Prize in Economic Sciences in Memory of Alfred Nobel 1971', *Nobelprize.org*, from <http://www.nobelprize.org/nobel_prizes/economic-sciences/laureates/1971/>, accessed on 4 February 2014.

channels interrupt regular programming to inform viewers that a nation's GDP for the quarter ended April has expanded by 1.2%. Social networks immediately explode with derision for the administration concerned.

GDP data has now come to mean so many, many things. Somehow, this obscure number has become a proxy for governance, business optimism and quality, social stability, pace of reform and global well-being. It even determines how we feel about ourselves, our families and our future lives. During an interview for a newspaper story a few years ago, I recall discussing government policy with an investment banker. Suddenly, he thumped his fist on the table and said: 'Boss! If India's GDP growth rate falls below 6%, people in this country start to die. Die!'

The general perception is that a bigger GDP is better than a smaller one. And a faster growing GDP is better than a slower growing one. Connect this with Angus Maddison's data on India's historical GDP numbers, and suddenly that 'India fact' starts looking extremely attractive. Maybe India was the richest country in the world.

There is just one problem. GDP numbers don't always imply wealth or social well-being.

And nobody knew it better than Kuznets himself. When presenting his original masterwork to the US Senate, Kuznets added a note of caution:

> The valuable capacity of the human mind to simplify a complex situation in a compact characterization becomes dangerous when not controlled in terms of definitely stated criteria… Measurements of national income are subject to this type of illusion and resulting abuse, especially since they deal with matters that are the centre of conflict of opposing

social groups where the effectiveness of an argument is often contingent upon oversimplification.[38]

In other words, Kuznets is already afraid that people—stupid, stupid, people—are going to misuse national income data, oversimplify the implications and use it to fiddle with society.

While Kuznets says that national income is a good way of measuring a nation's overall economic well-being, and of comparing the performances of various nations, this is merely surface analysis. It gives no indication of what lies beneath. He writes:

> Economic welfare cannot be adequately measured unless the personal distribution of income is known. And no income measurement undertakes to estimate the reverse side of income, that is, the intensity and unpleasantness of effort going into the earning of income. The welfare of a nation can, therefore, scarcely be inferred from a measurement of national income as defined above.[39]

This is a profound, foundational statement being made in the foundational document of national income accounting. Yet, for eight decades, this seems to be the part of the report that has reaped the least attention or introspection.

Little wonder then that Kuznets went on to become a leading researcher in developmental economics and was particularly passionate about helping poorer countries achieve economic well-being.

But if GDP itself isn't an adequate measure of the welfare of a nation's residents, is there a better metric?

[38]Simon Kuznets, 'National Income, 1929-1932', 73rd US Congress, Second session, Senate document no. 124, 1934, pp. 5-7.
[39]*Ibid.*

More importantly, for the Sceptics amongst us, is there a better way of justifying this 'India fact'? What other metric could we use to measure the economic welfare of the residents in pre-colonial India?

One measure Kuznets often used to distinguish between developed and less developed nations was per capita GDP. Or the national income of a country divided by its population. On the face of it, this makes sense. Large countries will naturally have a larger economy than smaller ones. But that doesn't automatically mean that the resident of a large country is better off than the resident of a small one, or vice versa. China is not 'richer' than San Marino or Monte Carlo or Kerala in any really meaningful way.

Per capita GDP, on the other hand, adjusts for population size. By averaging out income over the number of inhabitants, you could argue that it reflects the economic output of the average inhabitant.

Thankfully for us, Angus Maddison has a chart of historic per capita GDPs as well. Browse through this one, and suddenly things look different.

In 1 CE, Maddison estimates India's per capita GDP at $450 (1990 international dollar). This is in comparison to a global average of $467, an African average of $472 and a West European average of $576.

Fast forward to 1700, and India now has a per capita GDP of $550. By this point, world average has moved to $616 while West Europe has zoomed ahead to $997.

What happens next is...nothing. Under colonial rule, India simply stagnates. In fact, per capita GDP slips a little to $533 in the 1850s. And while it expands to $853 in 1973, by this point India has been overtaken by every major economy in the world save China.

The narrative as told by per capita GDP numbers is simple. India was reasonably wealthy around 2,000 years ago, but not exceptionally so. In the decades before the advent of the East India Company, India had already begun to lag behind several albeit smaller economies. And then colonialism delivers a crushing blow. India does not get much poorer, but it is forced to stand around and watch while much of the world zooms past.

Take the case of Japan. Japan and India were neck-and-neck almost till the moment of British supremacy. In 1700, Japan had a per capita GDP of $570 against India's $550. In 1913, Japan stood at $1387; India, meanwhile, languished at $673.

This undermines that original 'India fact' a little.

But there is just one more element that still irks me. And we must get that out of the way before our final pronouncements.

All this analysis is contingent on one crucial body of work: Angus Maddison's historical GDP estimates. All the narratives we've stitched together so far depend on Maddison's estimates.

But how in the world did he arrive at these numbers?

Maddison estimated two main groups of statistics that together gave us the famous charts: population and per capita GDP.

In a thirty-six-page appendix to *The World Economy: A Millennial Perspective*,[40] Maddison explains how he arrived at estimates for both population and per capita GDP for a host of nations. Where available, Maddison uses primary data. Next, he surveys estimates made by contemporary scholars and chooses the best one or an average of several good ones. If he finds no estimates at all, Maddison constructs his own based on whatever information he has available. There is, as you would expect, a fair bit of conjecture and extrapolation.

[40]Angus Maddison, *The World Economy: A Millennial Perspective* (Paris: OECD, 2001), Appendix C.

In the case of India's population, Maddison says that there is little reliable primary data available before the colonial period. So he picks one scholar's estimate for year 0 and the average of two scholars' estimates for year 1600. The latter is based on what the scholars calculate is the maximum size of population that India could have supported given its area under cultivation and productivity of farming methods. Maddison then fills in the gaps. For the modern period, of course, much better data is available.

The calculation of per capita GDP is based on even greater conjecture. Maddison calculates the per capita GDP required for subsistence levels of income as $400. (Again, the base currency here is the 1990 international dollar adjusted for price differences.) He also estimates that the per capita GDP levels for all of Asia, including India, was roughly the same as China from 0 to 1000 CE, that is, $450, adequately above subsistence to maintain a rich ruling class and some government.

For the Mughal period, Maddison uses an economic survey carried out during Akbar's administration. The rest of his analysis for India's economic growth from 1500 to 1850 CE is based off suggestions made by other researchers. The suggestions are, to put it mildly, conjectures more than estimates.

And then, on page 259, Maddison drops what I think is a moderate-sized bombshell. 'In all cases,' he says, 'GDP is derived by multiplying the per capita levels by the independently estimated levels of population.'

Wait. This sucks. A little bit. Essentially, this means that Maddison multiplied one estimate by another estimate to derive almost the entire part of his pre-colonial GDP chart for India.

So the primary reason why Maddison's data shows India to have the largest GDP in the ancient world is…India's population. That number multiplied by a per capita GDP moderately above subsistence, and growing very slowly, gives us a massive—and exceedingly approximate—figure for national income.

Which means that, as far as Maddison's data is concerned, this 'India fact' stands on very shaky ground indeed.

Still, there is much room for debate here. Was India wealthy? Undoubtedly. Was much of this wealth concentrated in the hands of very few people? Pretty much. (Maddison estimates that the Mughal court and aristocracy alone accounted for 15% of all consumption.) Did most of India's people live on little means? It looks like it. Was this very different from the rest of the world? Not really. At least, not till the seventeenth century. What changes India's fortunes is what happens afterwards.

This new narrative of Indian colonial economy has been my greatest learning in the course of this Sceptical investigation. To me, it seems that the British Empire's economic crime was not making a rich country poor but taking a somewhat moribund economy and keeping it that way while the rest of the world whooshed by.

The story of how that crime took place is interesting, infuriating and a little depressing. And not at all meant for this book.

So, the next time a trip to see the Crown Jewels in London, or maybe Tehran, tugs at your Indian heartstrings, chillax. They never really made that much of an economic difference anyway. Unless you are a descendant of Muhammad Shah. In which case, I would like to have a chat with you about a certain skirmish in Karnal.

SCEPTICAL PATRIOT INDIA FACT SCORECARD

Popular fact
India was the richest country in the world before the British came.

Score
5/10

Suggested fact
India has always been one of the largest economies in the world. And may have kept pace with the rest of the world if it hadn't been for colonial economic mismanagement to favour British industry.

Homework for the excessively sceptical
1. Angus Maddison's work throws up plenty of interesting and somewhat counter-intuitive ideas about the British impact on the Indian economy. For instance, he suggests that the British mildly reduced income inequality and vastly improves the reliability of agriculture. Explore with an open mind if possible.
2. We asked a few what-ifs in this chapter, chief of them being, what if the British never took over administration of India? How would the Indian economy have evolved under the Mughals?
3. In this book we have excessively focussed on Maddison's data and estimates. Are there another estimates? Do they paint a different picture?
4. I've met fiercely patriotic people who believe that if the Mughals had never invaded India, India may have developed along the lines of Japan as a major Asian economic and technological superpower. Others say

that India may have devolved into several smaller
nations. What do you think?

5. Are there lessons in the colonial experience for the
economists and policymakers of Independent India?
We can't change the past, but what mistakes can we
avoid in the future?

FIVE

The Talented, and Strange, Mr Bose

At some point between 20 and 22 July 1910, the captain of the *SS Montrose*, an ocean liner plying from Antwerp to Quebec, began to suspect that two of his passengers, one Mr John Robinson and his young son, were not who they were pretending to be. By his own recollection, later published in the *Daily Mail* newspaper, the captain said that he first realized that something was amiss when he spotted both passengers together on his deck one day, and noticed the son squeeze the father's hand 'immoderately'. 'It seemed to me unnatural of two males, so I suspected them at once.'[41]

His suspicions aroused, the shrewd captain, who some say fancied himself to be something of an amateur sleuth, began to observe the 'father and son' very closely. Very, very closely. The captain noted that the father read books such as *The Pickwick Papers*, *Neho the Nailer*, *Metropolis* and *A Name to Conjure With*.

The son, meanwhile, showed little indication of being a son at all: 'All the "boy's" manners at table when I was watching him were most lady like, handling knife and fork, and taking fruit off dishes with two fingers.' The captain even tried the oldest trick in the impostor-detection book: He waited for them to walk

[41]'Captain Kendall's Message', *Daily Mail*, 31 July 1910.

past, and then called after them with their presumed names. Several times Mr Robinson did not respond. And when he did, it was only after 'Master Robinson' prompted him.

By the 22nd, Captain Kendall was convinced: This was not Mr and Master Robinson, he concluded, but Dr Hawley Harvey Crippen and his lover, Ms Ethel le Neve—both wanted for a murder that had recently set all of Britain alight with morbid fascination. Crippen was believed to have murdered his wife and buried her body in the cellar of his house in London before fleeing with his secretary-cum-lover. That day, the captain asked one of the newest additions to his staff, his wireless operator, Lawrence Ernest Hughes, to radio a message to the authorities in Britain:

> Have strong suspicions that Crippen London cellar murderer and accomplice are among Saloon passengers. Moustache taken off—growing beard. Accomplice dressed as boy. Voice manner and build undoubtedly a girl.

Immediately, British police officers boarded an even faster ship, the *SS Laurentic*, and rushed across the Atlantic. They caught up with the *Montrose* just outside Quebec and boarded it under the guise of tugboat operators. Chief Inspector Walter Dew walked up to Mr Robinson, removed his tug cap, and is reported to have said with stereotypical English understatement: 'Good afternoon, Dr Crippen, remember me? I'm Inspector Dew with Scotland Yard.'[42]

Crippen, looking entirely relieved according to some witnesses, held up his hands to be cuffed. Four months later, on 23 November 1910, Crippen was executed at Pentonville Prison for the murder of his wife, Cora Henrietta Crippen.

---

[42]'Was Dr Crippen Innocent of His Wife's Murder?', *BBC News*, 29 July 2010.

The Crippen Cellar Murder has all the elements of a thrilling, timeless whodunit: The mysterious American homoeopathic doctor, his numerous affairs, his brazen crime of passion, the fleeing fugitives, the pathetic disguise, the chase by sea, and the dramatic apprehension just days before the criminal couple vanished into the endless expanses of Canada.

It is the kind of story, I suppose, that would play anywhere in the world with universal appeal, outrage and public scrutiny. But the Crippen case was also deeply entwined with, or at least drew a certain mystique from, the particular phase of human history in which it took place. It was a period of great industrial ingenuity, great leaps of scientific and engineering innovation and a period of rapid transformation in European government and society. It was also shortly before Europe was plunged into a brutal war that redrew national boundaries, rent asunder social structures and rewrote the fundamental social and moral rules by which millions of people in the continent lived their lives. It was a period of great global dislocation and universal loss of innocence.

Captain Kendall, for instance, went on to develop a certain reputation for indestructibility: Ship after ship sank with Kendall on board, yet the captain survived every single time. The ships involved in the story, the *Montrose* and the *Laurentic*, each went on to live their own eventful lives. One was blown away by a gale and foundered on a sandbank off the Kent coast. The *Laurentic*, pressed into military service, was sunk by mines, with millions of pounds of gold still in her hold.

Almost a century later, in 2007, the Crippen case re-emerged. Researchers discovered that the remains found in the cellar of the Crippen home in London may not have been that of Cora Crippen. In fact, it may not have been that of a woman at all. Was Dr Crippen wrongfully hanged? Or were his crimes not limited to just those of passion?

Yet, it is for none of these reasons that the Crippen murder case is most remembered today. It is most remembered, recalled and referenced for something else: Dr Crippen is believed to be the first ever criminal to be apprehended by means of a device that, at the time, was something of curious invention—the wireless radio.

It was curious for many, many reasons, not least of which was the fact that nobody, not even the pioneers of radio technology, really understood how it worked. But seldom in human history has an invention gone from the laboratory to the living room, as it were, as rapidly as the radio. Even by modern standards, the speed with which the radio was adopted into daily life was remarkable.

The fact that electric discharge could generate some sort of signal that could then be detected with a receiver was only discovered in 1879. By the late 1880s and early 1890s, several researchers had carried out only limited public demonstrations of wireless communication technology across any substantial distance. And yet, by the early 1900s, American magazines were already publishing directions for amateurs to build their own transmitters and receivers. By 1910, ships such as the *Montrose* were already employing wireless operators on long journeys. Two years later in 1912, records of telegraph communications were being used to analyze what exactly took place aboard the *Titanic*. Shortly after the *Titanic* sank, telegraph operators were employed on almost every ocean liner of note.

By the time the First World War became an entrenched, static, pointless meat-grinder of a mess, wireless operators were working in the trenches. One 1917 article in *Popular Science Monthly* told how operators at the frontline were often used to signal to men in the backward lines that clouds of poison gas had been unleashed towards them.[43]

[43] *Popular Science Monthly*, May 1917, pp. 795-99.

In just two decades, an invention had gone from being something of a circus spectacle and public amusement, to a messaging protocol reliable enough to be used on a field of battle. Such speed of adoption for new communication technology was perhaps unmatched till the Internet came along.

One man, more than any other, deserves credit for this mass propagation of new technology: Guglielmo Marconi. Marconi was an excellent engineer with a particular knack for understanding the commercial potential of complicated technology. He was also a spectacular showman with the twin abilities of making a big deal of what he understood and effortlessly glossing over what he did not.

So, while other scientists were fussing over the scientific underpinnings of how radio worked, Marconi was busy monetizing it. So much so that today Marconi is perhaps the best known of all the great 'inventors', along with Edison, Graham Bell and…err…Al Gore.

Yet, from the very beginning of Marconi's career, almost from the very moment he began filing his first patents, his claims have been disputed.

And one of the strongest claimants to the title of 'inventor of the radio', though perhaps he did not claim so with any vigour in his own life, was the great Indian scientist, teacher and pioneer Jagadish Chandra Bose.

Google the words 'Marconi Bose', and you'll unlock a world of impassioned, even outraged, debate. Dozens—hundreds, actually—of blog posts, essays and even academic papers put forth the claim that Bose was robbed. Everything from bad luck to racism has been blamed for the fact that instead of being held up as one of the greatest inventors of our time, J.C. Bose remains a middling celebrity in his own country and virtually unknown to the wider public outside.

So who invented the radio? Marconi? Or Bose?
This sounds like a job for the Sceptical Patriot.

✳✿✳

A long, long time ago, inside a lower middle-class apartment building far, far away in the United Arab Emirates of Abu Dhabi, a small fire broke out in a little built-in cupboard. The fire broke out at a particularly inconvenient time (not that there are ever any convenient times for fires to break out). Uncle, Aunty and their two daughters had all decided to return to India after spending decades in the UAE as expatriates. (Did they have a little son? Maybe they did. I don't remember these details. In any case, they are irrelevant.)

Half their apartment lay packed in cardboard boxes. The other half lay around in heaps, awaiting cardboard box-age. These included clothes, electronics, bottles of whisky and perfume... perfect fuel to escalate a little cupboard-sized fire into a full-fledged conflagration.

The fire broke out on a Thursday morning. Back in those days, in the early 1980s, most office-goers (but not schoolchildren) in the UAE worked five-and-a-half days a week before going home for the weekend around lunchtime on Thursday. So when Aunty began thumping on our door, her oversized nighty flapping around her, there were no 'men' around.

'What do I do? He is still in office! Diliala, do something!'

My mother, the above mentioned Diliala Sunny, was a remarkably resourceful woman. Within minutes, she popped next door, isolated the fire, removed all inflammable materials and arranged for a bucket brigade to douse the fire.

I don't want to sound overly pompous or anything, but my fearless fire-fighting accomplishments of that day are still spoken about with hushed tones of awe at Vadukut family gatherings. I was not even five-years-old at the time. Yet, I stood toe-to-toe with a raging four-foot tall fire that destroyed several books and a bag full of football boots. (No idea why they had a bag full of football boots, but I clearly remember looking on at the ruined husks of sporting equipment in wonder.)

Later that evening, after the men had come back from their offices, my parents and I popped over to see how our neighbours were doing. All that remained of the cupboard was a burnt-out cavity in the wall with a few charred books lying at the bottom. Uncle was tremendously grateful for our assistance. He was particularly appreciative of my individual inputs. He insisted that I be rewarded.

'What do you want, Sidin? Ask me for anything.'

I can still picture my mother standing there, holding her breath, waiting for me to say something utterly cringe-worthy.

Till that day, I had been something of an…eccentric child. I was called 'Reverse Gear' by some family friends because when I first began to crawl as a baby I could only do so backwards. Once, when another 'uncle' offered to buy me anything for a birthday or some such, I asked him for a large bag full of batteries (because all my toys had run out). Also, I once stabbed my dad in the face with a spoon, and another time I playfully punched an old neighbour man in the chest so hard that he had a mild cardiac event. All this before the age of five. I was like one of those Mensa child prodigies. Except that instead of being able to multiply two thirteen-digit numbers in three seconds, or learning seven languages by the age of three, my special ability was mortal carnage.

So there I stood, in the middle of a half-toasted bedroom, thinking of a suitable reward. My dad and mom quivered nearby. I slowly walked over to the black hole in the wall and peered at the detritus inside. No doubt my dad thought I was going to ask for one of the football boots.

'Uncle,' I said in a moment that completely changed my life, 'can I have one of those books?'

He sifted through the remains and pulled out the book that seemed the least damaged. It was one of those single volume encyclopaedias of the world that used to be a staple of bookstores everywhere till fifteen years ago, with names such as *Everything You Need to Know for Young Boy*s or *An Even Bigger Collection of Tell-Me-Whys!*

That book, half-toasted and smelling of ash, really did change my entire life. It made me love books, love reading, love history and appreciate science. It made me a lifelong gatherer of facts and data and, in particular, historical coincidences. It also made me a shameless book beggar, book borrower and book thief. It gave me an unusual—at least, I think it is unusual—propensity for remembering dates and timelines.

That book made me a better student in school and an easier child to my parents: Give me a book and an ice-cream cone, and I was maintenance-free for hours. Most of all, it made me curious. I wanted to know how satellites worked; why Iran and Iraq were fighting; and why, when India could get freedom from the British, it was bad for Khalistan to get freedom from India.

That was also the book that first introduced me to the idea of inventors and inventions. The very idea of 'inventing' something was just…amazing. How wondrous was this? One moment, something did not exist; the very next moment, somebody had conjured it into existence through sheer willpower. Nobody had televisions; John Logie Baird happened—and boom, televisions for everybody!

Or at least that is how I thought invention worked. You sat

around all day thinking and thinking, and EUREKA! Velcro! Shawarma!

When I was a child, I remember going through several phases of self-discovery. I spent a week being a patriotic poet, writing all kinds of hideous poems about Indian flags and Mahatma Gandhi and Param Vir Chakras. Then there was that prolonged period when I wanted to discover a new theorem in mathematics. Before all this was a period when I wanted to invent something. A board game, a banana-based dessert, anything. I just really, *really* wanted to be an inventor.

As I grew older, this childish urge went away. But there was no shortage of new inventors to discover. By which I mean memorize. Long lists of inventors and discoverers and authors and founders were central to every 'General Knowledge' curriculum in every school I ever went to.

Every 'General Knowledge' textbook had at least one chapter called 'Inventors' or 'Great Inventions', or even 'Inventors and Inventions'. This chapter was usually a dozen pages of text in two columns. Invention on the left. Inventor on the right. All set? Make yourself a cup of tea and commit the whole bloody thing to memory.

At the end of the term you had an exam featuring thought-provoking questions such as:

Who invented the automobile?
A) The Nazi party B) E.K. Nayanar C) Turnip
D) None of the above

The correct answer was, of course, A, B, C or D because the question was entirely wrong and the school would to give one free mark to everybody, provided they had attempted the question.

What I experienced was a hilarious approach to 'General

Knowledge' education that was all about committing useless information to memory without any coherent logical framework or context narrative.

This also means that legions of people now have a view of the process and history of 'inventing' that is utterly, utterly wrong. The long lists of inventions that most people commit to memory give them the perception that inventing is an individual exercise that results in sudden, yet complete, ready-to-market discoveries that instantly make the inventors concerned fabulously wealthy.

And few such perceptions are as wrong as the near-universally accepted notion that Guglielmo Marconi invented the radio.

He didn't.

Actually, it's complicated. Not just the invention itself. But also the history of wireless radio.

❈❈❈

A few years ago, I bought a tiny battery-powered FM/AM radio with earplugs. It is light enough to hang around my neck on a lanyard. I use it to listen to radio commentary when I go and see the occasional live sporting event. (I am so used to the chatter of on-screen commentators during televised sports that the comparative silence of live events freaks me out.)

The little blue and white device, about the same size as a large cigarette lighter but lighter, is perhaps the simplest electronic device I own. Yet, it is crammed to the gills with extremely complicated innovations. The plastic in the case, the transistors inside, even the synthetic fibre of the lanyard are all monumentally important inventions that have substantially changed the way we live our lives today. So there is little point in crediting one single individual for inventing the device in my pocket. It makes as much sense as calling Gandhi the inventor of India.

But what if we go back in time and start looking at primitive radio sets? Sets that came before plastic, and transistors and synthetic lanyards? Surely at some point somebody, maybe even Marconi, first thought of putting together the basic hardware required to make the first functioning radio broadcasting and receiving device?

The story of the invention of radio is really the story of the discovery of several component parts. First, of course, come the electromagnetic waves that form the medium of radio communication—this is heart of the whole business of wireless radio, or what my father would call the 'masala of the masala dosa'.

In 1865, the great Scot scientist James Clerk Maxwell published a paper titled 'A Dynamical Theory of the Electromagnetic Field'. Maxwell was a tremendously fecund scientist who, among other cool things, also managed to take one of the first stable colour photographs in history. However, it is perhaps for his work in electromagnetism that Maxwell is counted amongst the greatest scientists of all times. Maxwell, along with Einstein and Newton, completes the holy trinity of modern science.

Maxwell's work proved that electromagnetic fields move through space as waves with the same velocity of light. He also said that light was a form of electromagnetic wave itself, albeit one that was visible to the naked eye.

Maxwell never extended his work into figuring out how to, or if there was even a point in, actually transmitting and receiving these waves. But his equations remain at the heart of wireless communication to this day.

He also helped create an entirely brand new avenue of research for a whole generation of scientists. Soon others began to wonder what other types of electromagnetic waves were there besides light. Later they began to wonder if perhaps these waves could be generated and broadcast at will.

In the two decades after Maxwell's initial work, there were a great many baby steps taken towards the ultimate realization of wireless communication. All over the world, from Brazil to Europe and even further, scientists tinkered away at the parts that formed the whole: transmitters, detector, receivers, antenna, lenses...

But the next great Maxwellian step, if you will, in this story was taken by Heinrich Rudolf Hertz. Science's way of rewarding its really great practitioners is to name units of measurements after them. To this day, radios measure and display frequencies in hertz, often using the abbreviation 'hz'. This adequately represents the man's position in science history.

While Maxwell had provided the theoretical framework for the propagation of electromagnetic waves, Hertz did the experimental heavy-lifting. So important was his work that in the early years of wireless telegraphy there was even a movement to name the technology after him. In the preface to his 1902 book, *Wireless Telegraphy: A Popular Exposition*, author G.W. de Tunzelmann writes about the name of the technique:

> I should be inclined to suggest the term Hertz Wave Tellegraphy or Hertzian Telegraphy for the system of telegraphic without connecting wires which is now exciting so much interest and attention. Though greatly developed by the researches of Lodge, Marconi, and others, Hertzian telegraph depends upon exiting at the transmission station and detecting at a distant receiving station ether waves of a certain character, the existence of which had been deduced theoretically by Professor Clerk Maxwell, but first experimentally demonstrated by the late Dr Hertz, of Carlsruhe, who published the results in a series of papers in the *Widemann's Annalen* beginning in July, 1887.[44]

[44] G.W. de Tunzelmann, *Wireless Telegraphy: A Popular Exposition* (London: Office of "Knowledge", 1901), pp. 9-10.

Besides highlighting Hertz's role in the development of radio, I reproduced that excerpt here for a couple of more reasons. First of all, it indicates that as early as 1902 there was already consternation about whom to credit for the concept of wireless radio. Secondly, even at this stage, well-informed people didn't really get how the radio worked. Note the author's use of the term 'ether waves', a now discredited idea that the universe was filled with a substance called ether that conveyed light and many other waves.

There is no disputing Hertz's pivotal role at this point. Hertz wrote about and, more importantly, demonstrated his system for sending and receiving waves. Unfortunately, he also came to the conclusion that his system of wireless transmission and reception had no practical, and therefore no commercial, application. This must go down as one of history's great miscalculations. But to be fair to Hertz, this could also be because at the time his apparatus was incapable of sending signals over any great distance.

Also, this was not a viewpoint that was unique to Hertz. Many pioneers involved in the early history of wireless telegraphy simply did not recognize the business potential of the technology. Or, if they did, they didn't seem to care.

The onus of converting Maxwell's theory and Hertz's experimental work into a booming, international business empire fell to Guglielmo Marconi, a young Italian man with a great aptitude for science but an even greater ability for application.

The general view is that Marconi read Hertz's work, spotted the shortcomings that prevented radio from being a viable alternative to wired telegraphy, and began chipping away at these roadblocks.

At the same time, across the Atlantic, another scientist, engineer and all-round oddball, the great Nikola Tesla, began experimenting with radio as well. In addition to both these well-known names, a number of lesser-known figures were furiously testing, calculating and even demonstrating.

If you had to plot the history of radio along a timeline, and tried to include every single big and small development, it would basically feature three milestones separated by a dense smattering of smaller improvements. Maxwell's equations were the first milestone and Hertz's experiments second. Now all that remained was the third: a major public demonstration of radio communication across long distances.

Several scientists had demonstrated the ability to transmit and receive radio waves across short distances within laboratories. But as soon as they tried to transmit over longer distances, they ran into trouble. There were several challenges. And most of them clearly outside the purview of this leisurely book. However, we shall talk about one of the most important conundrums: how to accurately detect incoming signals?

The longer the distances you tried to cover, the more sensitive your receivers had to be. The first great breakthrough in this field came with the development of a device known as the coherer. The credit for this is generally given to Frenchman Edouard Branly. In 1890, Branly discovered that exposing a small container loosely packed with metal filings to radio transmission changed their electrical properties. Usually the filings were too loosely packed to conduct electricity; but when exposed to radio waves these filings began to stick together, or cohere, and become much better conductors. Now all you had to do was hook up a coherer to a source of electric current and place it in the path of radio waves. As soon as waves hit the filings, a current began to flow.

Branly's design was later picked up by other scientists, especially Sir Oliver Lodge, who then improved its functioning and its sensitivity.

Marconi's genius was his ability to see the big picture. While other scientists worked on individual pieces of the radio puzzle, Marconi simultaneously began to drop each piece into its rightful place. Along the way, he also became something of a patent troll. Indeed, Marconi was perhaps the first great technology entrepreneur to use patents and relentless legislation to expand and secure his business interests. Throughout his life, Marconi acquired and protected patents with great zeal. After his life, his businesses continued to do so.

While other scientists were happy demonstrating their radio kits in lecture halls and classrooms, Marconi directly approached the men who ran Britain's postal system and armed forces. After demonstrating his technology over short distances on the roof of the GPO building in London, in late 1896 Marconi carried out his first great outdoor demonstration. Between 1 and 11 September 1896, Marconi was able to transmit and receive signals over a distance of almost two miles. By all accounts, the equipment he used was a mishmash—brilliant, but a mishmash nonetheless—of ideas and devices introduced by a whole list of pioneers, including Tesla and Branly. This did not prevent Marconi from claiming that the technology was entirely of his own making.

Later, Marconi carried out a number of public demonstrations in London that would have made Steve Jobs proud. For instance, Marconi would walk around a room, through a packed audience, carrying a box with a bell inside. On stage, William Preece, an engineer with the British postal service, would operate a transmitter. Each time a signal was sent, the bell inside would ring. The response was uproarious. Local newspapers began reporting these lectures and demonstrations. Marconi became a star.

Guglielmo Marconi, however, took things one step further. In July 1897, shortly after securing a patent titled 'Improvements in Transmitting Electrical Impulses and Signals and in Apparatus Thereof', Marconi formed a company called the Wireless Telegraph and Signal Company. This was the kind of audacity that would impress some of the dot-com boom's most adventurous billionaires. (By which I mean, the guys whose business plans weren't worth the paper they were printed on.)

It was audacious because Marconi set up a company that would make and sell radio equipment despite having technology that was experimental at best, intellectual property of dubious originality, and practically no clients. Its roots may have been precarious, but in one form or the other this company would last for more than a century.

As soon as he began to make money, Marconi began to face questions and legal disputes. Tesla, for instance, had a prolonged rivalry with him over many of his patents and innovations. When Marconi achieved his *coup de grace* of all demonstrations, a transatlantic transmission in December 1901, from Poldhu Wireless Station in Cornwall, England, to Signal Hill in St John's Newfoundland, Canada, Tesla claimed that the achievement piggy-backed on at least seventeen of his own patents.

It was a rivalry that would end very differently for both men. Tesla died in a hotel room in New York, discredited and penniless. Marconi won the Nobel Prize in 1909, received knighthoods and national honours, expanded his network of companies all over the world and became extremely rich. Benito Mussolini was the best man at Marconi's wedding. And when he died, he received a state funeral in Rome.

Marconi also found his way into general knowledge textbooks all over the world as the 'inventor of the radio'. This labelling is an act of historical and scientific reductionism that does great disservice to the dozens of other enterprising investigators on whose shoulders Marconi stood.

Yet, as recently as 1998, researchers were still figuring out how much Marconi had depended on the inventions of others. In January that year, Dr Probir K. Bondyopadhyay published a paper titled 'Sir J.C. Bose's Diode Detector Received Marconi's First Transatlantic Wireless Signal of December 1901'.

The paper explained, in detail that seems to satisfy many subsequent commentators, that the success of Marconi's seminal Signal Hill transatlantic transmission of 1901—one that boosted his profile and business internationally—was owed in large part to a type of coherer that had originally been designed by the Indian scientist Jagadish Chandra Bose. Instead of metal filings, Bose's design used a drop of mercury.

Bose first presented the idea for an iron-mercury-iron coherer at the Royal Society in London in 1899. It then promptly fell out of public attention until it resurfaced again, two years later, as part of Marconi's receiving equipment in Newfoundland. There was immediately a minor scandal over the provenance of this mercury coherer. Marconi insisted that the coherer had been gifted to him by a childhood friend. Sceptics kept pushing. And the story gets murkier and murkier. Unfortunately, J.C. Bose and his original design appear to have been forgotten entirely by this time. Instead, people kept asking Marconi: 'Where did you get this coherer from? What are you hiding?'

What makes Marconi's claim all the more dubious is an excerpt from a letter that Bose wrote to his friend and admirer, Rabindranath Tagore in 1901. In this, he referred to an incident that took place shortly before a lecture at the Royal Society in London on 17 May 1901.

> A short time before my lecture, a multi-millionaire proprietor of a very famous telegraph company telegraphed me with an urgent request to meet me. I replied that I had no time. In

response he said that he is coming to meet me in person and within a short time he himself arrived with patent forms in hand. He made an earnest request to me not to divulge all valuable research results in today's lecture: 'There is money in it, let me take out patent for you. You do not know what money you are throwing away', etc. Of course, 'I will only take half share in the profit, I will finance it', etc.

This multi-millionaire has come to me like a beggar for making some more profits. Friend, you would have seen the greed and hankering after money in this country— money, money—what a terrible all-pervasive greed! If I once get sucked into this terrible trap, there won't be any escape! See, the research that I have been dedicated to doing is above commercial profits. I am getting older—I am not getting enough time to do what I had set out to do. I refused him.[45]

It was a noble, if fateful, decision. Some people believe that if Bose had stated his claim to the device in more concrete terms— say, with a patent—he would have become a much more famous man. A Rabindranath Tagore of science. He may have also got very close to a Nobel Prize.

This is all conjecture. What we do know today, with considerable certainty, is that one of the greatest triumphs in modern communications sciences was made possible by an Indian scientist's insight.

Yet, there is more to the great Bose 'India fact', a much more fundamental claim to Marconi's throne. There is proof that Jagadish Chandra Bose demonstrated long-range wireless communication in front of a live audience even before the great Guglielmo Marconi.

[45]Personal letter from J. C. Bose to Rabindranath Tagore, 17 May 1901.

However, before you go any further, I'd like to point out one aspect of this chapter so far that bothers me somewhat. That quote from Bose's letter to Tagore that I included above is quite popular with Bose aficionados and India fact enthusiasts, for obvious reasons. It gives Bose's eccentric personality a certain virtuous, intellectual sincerity.

Despite my best efforts, however, I have been unable to trace it to an original source. Even though the quote appears in numerous books, they all seem to refer to each other or to other versions of this quote, but never the original source itself. Also the timing of the letter seems a little odd. Bose's lectures at the Royal Society in 1901 had nothing to do with radio communication. By this point, he had switched his interest to the world of plants.

This does not materially impact the rest of this chapter in any way. And even if this quote is a fabrication, it does not take away from Bose's fundamental approach to sciences and research.

Still, I just thought that you should know.

※☆※

Jagadish Chandra Bose was one of the great Indian scientific minds of the late nineteenth and early twentieth century. Born to a Bengali civil servant of a distinctly bohemian bent of mind, Bose had a colourful, if somewhat conflicted, childhood. Reading through writings about Bose's youth, both by himself and other people, one gets the feeling that his family tried to strike a balance between enjoying the benefits bestowed by the British and the earthy wisdom of India's villages. This did not come without sacrifices.

One biography of Bose, written in his lifetime by a close acquaintance, speaks of an incident that took place shortly after Bose was enrolled in St Xavier's School in Calcutta. Mostly populated by English city boys, Bose was subjected to severe bullying.

> Heavily pounded accordingly, with bleeding nose and dazed and watery eyes he seemed defeated and the fight practically at an end; but then came a burst of war-fury, a memory perhaps of the old heroes, at any rate an onslaught so furious as to surprise the other, and knock him down, well nigh stunned, and unwilling or unable to rise at call. So the youngster was hailed victor, and acquired full rights of freemanship; yet hardly of comradeship, for the respective backgrounds of town and country, of East Bengal and England, remained too different.[46]

This is an incident that seems to play out, over and over again, throughout his life: the outsider battling to fit in and take what is rightfully his. Except that, as he grew older, intellectual horsepower and sheer resilience instead of fists became his weapons.

Bose was never an exceptional student, in India or later in England, where he acquired degrees from Cambridge and the University of London. It was only after he returned to India in 1885, and became a professor of physics at Presidency College in Calcutta, that he really bloomed into an intellectual inquisitor.

Despite arriving from England with several letters of recommendation, Bose appears to have been treated very shabbily indeed by the Indian educational establishment. He was given a post and salary unbefitting his qualifications. In protest, a miffed Bose worked for three years without drawing any salary at all. Eventually, the authorities relented and paid him at par with his English colleagues.

[46]Sir Patrick Geddes, *The Life and Work of Sir Jagadis C. Bose* (New York: Longmans, Green & Co, 1920), p. 21.

Nine years after his return from England, on his thirty-fifth birthday, Bose made a vow: He would now 'start regular work as an investigator'.[47] And for his area of investigation Bose chose the most 'conspicuous movement in physics' of the time—electric waves.

Just one year later, in 1894, at the Town Hall in Calcutta, Bose carried out an experiment that has since become the stuff of Indian science legend. He set up a radio transmitter in one room, and a receiver three rooms and seventy-five feet away. In between, posing as a hurdle to the signal, were three walls and the lieutenant governor of Calcutta. To boost the power of this radio system, Bose equipped both the transmitter and the receiver with 'an apparatus which curiously anticipated the lofty "antennae" of modern wireless telegraphy—a circular metal plate at the top of a 2-foot pole'.[48]

Bose's system was strong enough for the receiver to have enough energy to ring a bell, discharge a pistol and explode a 'miniature mine'.

Of course, this pre-dates any of Marconi's long-range demonstrations. In fact, many people believe that this is the first true demonstration of wireless radio across any distance and through obstacles.

Now, the conventional narrative is that, despite this headstart, Marconi, and not Bose, has always been given credit for the first major public demonstration and, subsequently, the 'invention of radio'. This is not exactly true.

During his career, Bose visited England several times and made numerous extremely well-received demonstrations of his own radio transmission abilities. These were widely covered in

[47] *Ibid.*, p. 47.
[48] *Ibid.*, pp. 61-65.

newspapers and magazines. In March 1897, *McClure's Magazine*, an American illustrated monthly, featured a fascinating article titled 'Telegraphing Without Wires: A Possibility of Electrical Science'. Uniquely, it featured interviews with both Bose and Marconi. In the article, the author referred to Bose as the 'discoverer' of this 'new telegraphy'.

The real question, then, is not why Bose isn't credited for the discovery of radio or playing an important role in it. The real question is: How did everyone forget?

One indication is in the *McClure's* article. 'He disliked publicity in the extreme,' it says about Bose.

> To be interviewed for publication, and to have his delicate, complex and ultra-technical work described in the non-technical language of a popular magazine is something from which he shrinks visibly.[49]

Marconi, on the other hand, had no qualms about admitting his lack of credentials as a scientist. When the reporter asked him the difference between his waves and Hertz's waves, Marconi said:

> I don't know. I am not a scientist but I doubt if any scientist can yet tell. I have a vague idea that the difference lies in the form of the wave. I could tell you a little more clearly if I could give you the details of my transmitter and receiver. They are now being patented, however, and I cannot say anything about them.[50]

These were two radically different approaches to talking about one's work. Bose believed in talking about his science only if he

[49]H. J. W. Dam, 'Telegraphing Without Wires: A Possibility of Electrical Science', *McClure's Magazine*, March 1897, pp. 383-92.
[50]*Ibid.*

had to—and that too only in terms that did complete justice to its scientific content. He didn't like watering it down. He also didn't like talking about commercial applications or patents. He probably abhorred commercialization.

Marconi spoke about science in vague—some might even say 'popular'—terms. He was also secretive. This, no doubt, helped serve two purposes. First, it made him sound like a miracle worker, a mystic. Secondly, it bought him the time to patent everything and anything. It also helped make him the ideal media celebrity: young, handsome, easy to understand, accessible and mysterious enough without being mystifying.

Marconi beat Bose, and everybody else working in radio, at the media and business games. In the long term, this meant that Marconi's name became synonymous with radio technology.

There was one more thing, which was perhaps the final straw. Bose's dalliance with radio technology was exceedingly brief. Suddenly, almost overnight, he swung all his powers of investigation and experimentation to the area of biophysics. From the early 1900s onwards, Bose began to investigate what he called 'Response in the Living And Non-Living'. Noticing parallels in the way living and non-living things reacted to electrical and various other stimuli, Bose began to wonder how far these parallels went. Did plants react, for instance, to temperature and corrosive fluids in the same way that metals did? Was there a way to measure these reactions precisely?

Bose committed the rest of his productive life to this course of work. It made him moderately famous, took him around the world, and seems to have satisfied him deeply in the early days. But it took him far, far away from his work and legacy in radio. And, sadly for Bose, it looks like his work in biophysics, whilst interesting, was never as path-breaking as his work with radio transmission, and antenna or coherer design. And, in the latter part of his career, international audiences began to treat him with less and less respect. His papers began to get ignored, his work undermined, his research set aside. At a time when science seems to have got more and more obsessed with application and engineering, Bose's work—measuring the sensitivities and memories of plants, for instance—seemed to occupy a certain metaphysical realm.

As for radio, he vacated the space completely, letting others such as Marconi usurp the limelight.

Towards the end of his career, Bose spent more and more time working as an educational administrator and institution builder. The Bose Institute in Calcutta was founded in his time, and functions to this day, with a stellar reputation for interdisciplinary work.

So, did Bose really invent the radio before Marconi?

The problem with this question is…the question.

Wireless communication is the end-product of decades of innovation by dozens of scientists. There is little doubt that calling Marconi the inventor of radio does him excessive credit; several dozens of inventions made radio possible. Calling Marconi 'the father of radio' makes a lot more sense. If it wasn't for his relentless energy in applying the science, his flair for demonstration, and his hunger to commercialize wireless radio, it could have well taken several more years for wireless to become a worldwide messaging platform. Or, perhaps, Tesla would have propagated it instead. We will never know for sure.

What about Bose? Bose's mercury coherer played a central role in the single most important demonstration in wireless radio history. His own demonstration was one of the earliest— if not *the* earliest—displays of long-range wireless transmission in history.

He was one of a handful of pivotal figures in the history

of wireless radio. Yet, he was not the sole inventor or the only father. Neither was Marconi.

SCEPTICAL PATRIOT INDIA FACT SCORECARD

Popular fact
Jagadish Chandra Bose invented the radio before Marconi.

Score
6/10

Suggested fact
Jagadish Chandra Bose was one of the pivotal researchers in the golden age of wireless research. His experimental work was outstanding at a global level, and unsurpassed at a national level. And if it wasn't for his invention of the mercury coherer, Marconi's greatest ever public demonstration of the radio may not have been possible. In a country that has a poor record for pure science research, J.C. Bose is a giant among men.

Homework for the excessively sceptical
1. How important was Bose's work in biophysics? Are there any great forgotten discoveries lurking there?
2. How about a day-trip to the Bose Institute? Some of his original equipment is carefully preserved there.
3. Why do douchebags like Marconi always seem to get all the credit?
4. How many other 'inventors' made a fortune on the uncredited works of others?
5. Did you know that C.V. Raman once referred to some of Bose's metaphysical work as 'mumbo-jumbo'? Investigate.

SIX

The Best Language

Don't you just love how far technology has come in our lifetimes?

I remember, as an NRI child in the Middle East, watching science and technology documentaries with rapt attention. (In fact, mostly I remember spending hour upon hour adjusting our TV aerial one nanometre a time till we got a half-decent signal from the best TV channel in the world: Saudi Arabia 2. God, I miss Saudi Arabia 2. At that age, you didn't get the impression at all that this was a nation that beheaded people on the weekends for fun.)

There was one particular episode of a show that is burnt into my brain like footsteps on wet concrete. The host, after some suitably engrossing banter, drops the handset of one of those old-fashioned bakelite telephones onto a cradle. The contraption then makes some energetic wildlife-like noises before going quiet. 'This computer,' the man says, 'is now online. And connected to an international network of computers.'

All my subsequent thoughts were in upper case.

WHAT MADNESS IS THIS! A NETWORK OF COMPUTERS! ALL CONNECTED! GLOBALLY! AND I HAVE AN ATARI WITH THAT STUPID BOXING GAME WHERE YOU CAN ONLY SEE THE HEADS AND THE HANDS OF THE TWO BOXERS AND YOU PUNCH AND PUNCH LIKE A FOOL!

Yet…yet, look at how far we've come in the last two decades. I am writing this chapter on an 11-inch Macbook Air computer that is connected, via a wireless network, to millions of other computing devices…in just my living room. And if these hardware achievements are astonishing, the software and applications we use these days are astonishing-er still.

Nothing impresses me more than a mobile phone's miraculous ability to make out what I am saying to it. Recently, my sister-in-law bought herself an iPhone 5, with that magical voice-activated feature called Siri. She can now, literally, ask her iPhone to find things for her. For instance, if she feels a sudden craving for pizza, all she has to do is press a button and say: 'Find me pizza places nearby.' Within moments, Siri will record her command, translate that into a query, process this query through a search engine, find the answers, process that, and then, in a magical voice, say: 'The current temperature on Wednesday is 32.45 Yen.'

Sheer computing magic.

Ok, ok, I exaggerate. Siri actually does a pretty decent job of this kind of thing.

But what most people don't often realize is the mind-boggling complexity of this simple Siri process. Without knowing any advanced computer science engineering, we can appreciate the fact that dozens of computers and servers are used to process our pizza query. An entire chain of computers transmits our query across the globe to a search engine company's server, where it passes through an entire farm of servers before finding an answer, and then hitches a ride back to our iPhone via several other computers.

And yet, I've come to realize recently that the most complicated part of the process may not be any of these things. No. The most computationally challenging aspect of this information supply chain is—or, at least, used to be—trying to make out what you're telling the phone. And then figuring out how to give you the response in sensible language.

One of my cousins has a small son who is just about old enough to speak rudimentary sentences. Just about, but not quite. Yet, he is a precocious child who loves communicating. Watching him speak is utterly fascinating. You can almost hear his brain cells firing as he puts together word after word, the veins in his neck straining with the effort, before spitting out his sentences. My cousin and his wife are worried that he might be speaking a little too much for a child his age.

But I find him captivating. Watching him both learn and, in a sense, create his language, is intriguing. It is—pardon the cliché—like watching a human being take shape right before your eyes.

In just a few years, though, and this is the incredible bit, he will speak with the fluency of a grown-up. Of course, his vocabulary will develop over time. But he already understands the complex syntax of at least one and often many more languages.

Human beings develop this skill almost instinctively.

For computers, however, language is a completely different matter.

Despite what your Google search box, or Siri-enabled phone, might lead you to believe, computers need a lot of help to make sense of the language that human beings like you and me so casually communicate with.

This ability, usually called natural language processing, remains a huge challenge and an area of relentless exploration for information technology companies. One Google corporate website lists 197 publications by Google engineers just in the area of NLP (Neuro-Linguistic Programming) over the last decade, almost two a month. And some of the most recent of these publications suggests that understanding human speech remains a significant hurdle for machines. This despite the fact that some of the world's brightest computer scientists have been working on natural language processing for over seven decades.

In 1985, one such scientist published a paper in the spring issue of *The AI Magazine*, the official quarterly of the Association for the Advancement of Artificial Intelligence (AAAI).

Never in the history of 'India facts' had a single document spurned so many India facts, so quickly.

✻✧✻

On 5 January 1954, American computer makers, IBM published a press release that stunned the world.

> Russian was translated into English by an electronic 'brain' today for the first time.
>
> Brief statements about politics, law, mathematics, chemistry, metallurgy, communications and military affairs were submitted in Russian by linguists of the Georgetown University Institute of Languages and Linguistics to the famous 701 computer of the International Business Machines Corporation. And the giant computer, within a few seconds, turned the sentences into easily readable English.
>
> A girl who didn't understand a word of the language of the Soviets punched out the Russian messages on IBM cards. The 'brain' dashed off its English translations on an automatic printer at the breakneck speed of two and a half lines per second.[51]

[51]'701 Translator', IBM Press Release, 8 January 1954, from <http://www-03.ibm.com/ibm/history/exhibits/701/701_translator.html>, accessed on 4 February 2014.

The press release then quoted one of the researchers:

> Although he emphasized that it is not yet possible 'to insert
> a Russian book at one end and come out with an English
> book at the other,' Doctor Dostert predicted that 'five,
> perhaps three years hence, interlingual meaning conversion
> by electronic process in important functional areas of several
> languages may well be an accomplished fact.'

It was a prediction that would go on to haunt everyone associated
with the 'Georgetown Experiment'. Because even ten years
after that original demonstration, machines were no closer to
electronically translating languages. Funding for research into
machine translation—which had poured in after that much
hyped demo—dried up rapidly.

Bombastic press release and international media hype
notwithstanding, the Georgetown Experiment was something
of a showpiece. The 701 IBM computer had been programmed
with a very small vocabulary and just a handful of grammar
rules. And the sentences that had been fed into the machine had
been specially 'chosen' for the occasion.

Decades later, we are still no closer to feeding a Russian book
into a computer and getting an English translation back.

Why is it so damn hard to get computers to understand
you? Especially if they seem so capable of doing everything else,
including landing a passenger plane or bringing a space vehicle
back into the earth's atmosphere at precise angles and velocities?

I am going to try to tell you. Mind you, I will be standing on
very thin ice while I do so. Natural language processing is the
kind of discipline that gets very technical very, very quickly. And
I am going to take narrative liberties to criminal extents.

Computers, washing machines, the latest smart phones
function according to a set of rules loaded into them in some

way. These rules can get complicated enough to look human, or even magical. Notice how Gmail can tell the difference between spam email and a good email with nearly perfect accuracy. Some computers are even capable of dynamically creating new rules to help them function better. Search engines, for instance, try to throw up results based on the kinds of links you've clicked on before.

All very magical indeed. But all, nonetheless, based on a very, very elaborate set of rules, information and dependencies.

The same thing goes for the way we all process language. When the missus tells us, 'Why haven't you bought milk yet?' a countless number of processes kick off in our heads. We process the meaning of her words, her tone of voice, the context in which she has said it, and several other environmental variables, before we arrive at our interpretation of what she has said. We do this instinctively. But getting computers to do this is exceedingly hard.

In the early years of NLP technology, computers were fed with grammatical rules and dictionaries to help them interpret sentences, and perhaps translate them into other languages. As you may have guessed, this work went hand-in-hand with the development of technologies like artificial intelligence techniques.

But these primitive methods of dictionary look-ups didn't work well enough. Soon researchers realized that they needed a much broader and deeper set of rules that would help computers understand the meaning *and* syntax of sentences. In other words, both what the words meant and how the sentence was spoken.

An excellent overview of the history of NLP is an October 2001 paper by Karen Sparck Jones of the University of Cambridge, titled 'Natural Language Processing: A Historical Review'. By the late 1970s, Jones wrote, NLP researchers had moved into a grammato-logical phase. Piggybacking on the work of some pioneering linguists, computer scientists began working with the grammar and logic of languages to create a framework of rules that computers could use to parse sentences.

The analogy of the tourist phrasebook may work here. In the early years, computers were like tourists trying to speak a foreign language using only a phrasebook and an English-Foreign dictionary. Then, in this grammato-logical phase, they were given some rudimentary textbooks with grammar lessons in them.

But the internal processes within these machines still amounted to breaking down a sentence into a few pieces—meaning, grammar, logic—that could then be understood through an elaborate framework of rules and relationships.

The problem was that languages in the real world didn't function that way. They didn't function according to neat little grammato-logical frameworks. Artificial languages, the ones such as Basic or Pascal or Fortran, used to programme computers did, but not the ones the average guy on the street spoke.

The simple English phrase, 'screw you', for instance, can mean so many things to different people depending on how you say it, where you say it and who is saying it to whom:

1. 'Piss off, you little shit.'
2. 'I will make sweet love to you.'
3. 'I will have a screw. And you?'
4. 'What driver is a cocktail of orange juice and vodka, you ask?'

Now, asking a machine to translate this 'screw you' to Russian or Italian would drive it…insane.

But what if you turned this question on its head? What if,

instead of trying to create a super-complex framework that could parse a language, you tried to find a language that already had a super-complex framework of rules for grammar and logic?

Researchers began to wonder…if only there was a 'street' language that already had a strong set of rules that machines could parse immediately.

And that is exactly what Rick Briggs suggested in his 1985 *AI Magazine* paper titled 'Knowledge Representation in Sanskrit and Artificial Intelligence'.

> Understandably, there is a widespread belief that natural languages are unsuitable for the transmission of many ideas that artificial languages can render with great precision and mathematical rigor.
>
> But this dichotomy, which has served as a premise underlying much work in the areas of linguistics and artificial intelligence, is a false one. There is at least one language, Sanskrit, which for the duration of almost 1,000 years was a living spoken language with a considerable literature of its own. Besides works of literary value, there was a long philosophical and grammatical tradition that has continued to exist with undiminished vigour until the present century. Among the accomplishments of the grammarians can be reckoned a method for paraphrasing Sanskrit in a manner that is identical not only in essence but in form with current work in Artificial Intelligence. This article demonstrates that a natural language can serve as an artificial language also, and that much work in AI has been reinventing a wheel millennia old.[52]

Briggs's idea is captivating. Thanks to centuries of rigorous work and study, Sanskrit has a rich grammatical tradition.

[52]'Knowledge Representation in Sanskrit and Artificial Intelligence', *AI Magazine* , Vol. 6, 1985, pp. 22-38.

Briggs suggested that this made Sanskrit, with its elaborate superstructure of grammato-logical rules, function much like an artificial machine-friendly language. In other words, Sanskrit would be much easier than most other languages for a computer to parse.

Also, by studying the grammar of the Sanskrit language more closely, Briggs suggested, computer scientists might even find ways of creating better artificial languages and machine parsers. After all, Sanskrit schools had already spent centuries on the grammato-logical foundations of the language.

Briggs's paper ends on a very lofty note:

> It is interesting to speculate as to why the Indians found it worthwhile to pursue studies into unambiguous coding of natural language into semantic elements. It is tempting to think of them as computer scientists without the hardware, but a possible explanation is that a search for clear, unambiguous understanding is inherent in the human being. Let us not forget that among the great accomplishments of the Indian thinkers were the invention of zero and of the binary number system a thousand years before the West re-invented them. Their analysis of language casts doubt on the humanistic distinction between natural and artificial intelligence, and may throw light on how research in AI may finally solve the natural language understanding and machine translation problems.

Briggs's paper quite possibly became the most widely quoted research document in the history of Independent India. But not immediately. At first, there was instant interest but largely within academic circles in India. Linguists, historians, computer scientists…everyone found it a platform to delve more deeply into Sanskrit.

The very year after Briggs's paper was published, the Computer Society of India organized the 'First National Conference on Knowledge Representation and Inference in Sanskrit' in Bengaluru from 20 to 22 December. Briggs attended the conference, along with Indian scientists and several Sanskrit scholars. Later, in 1987, Briggs published a brief one-page report on the conference for *AI Magazine*, which makes for interesting reading.

By my reckoning, this First Conference was the only one on the topic. But it did spawn plenty of research initiatives into Sanskrit grammar and NLP that continue to go on in Indian institutions. The conference report was also the last piece that Rick Briggs ever wrote for *AI Magazine*.

Which means, in all likelihood, the original Briggs paper would have eventually been forgotten by everybody except for a small number of NLP researchers and Sanskrit geeks in India and abroad.

But then, in the early years of the twenty-first century, the Internet happened. And with it came a lot of Indian users eager to latch on to any good 'India fact'.

Today the Briggs paper enjoys a second life as the fountainhead of not just one but several 'India facts'. Somehow, the paper seems to generate a new piece of trivia every few years, as if the truth is massaged out of it by blogger after patriotic blogger. The most recent one was that NASA had launched a 'Mission Sanskrit' to educate thousands of American students in the most scientific of all languages.

NASA has done no such thing.

Before that, there was the 'fact' that Sanskrit was better than C, C++ and JAVA for computer programming.

This fact later evolved into the one where Sanskrit had been announced as the 'best language in the world'. On some lists this proclamation is attributed to the European Union. On other lists, the claim to Sanskrit's greatness dates back to a *Forbes* magazine report from July 1987. As far as I know there is no such report. Then there is the claim that NASA has bestowed this honour upon Sanskrit. (It is truly remarkable how NASA has become the 'India fact' certifying agency of choice.)

Whatever be the source for this India fact, the conclusions are usually the same.

1: Ancients in India had discovered artificial intelligence thousands of years before anybody else in the West.

2: Sanskrit is the best language for programming computers in the world.

What about the original paper that unleashed all this glory and triumph?

In most cases, Rick Briggs is credited as the 'NASA scientist' who discovered Sanskrit's AI properties. In fact, in the original 1985 paper, Briggs is identified as working for 'RIACS, NASA Ames Research Center, Moffet Field, California 94305'. RIACS stands for the Research Institute for Advanced Computer Science, an institution that supplies NASA with computing inputs for space missions. (The most ludicrous reference to Rick Briggs I have found anywhere was that he was 'head of the Vedic Mathematics Cell at NASA'. I checked the NASA website: They seem to have no such cell.)

There is one problem with all this, though. On page eight of the same 1987 issue of *AI Magazine* in which the conference report appears, the editors published brief biographies of all the contributors. This is what they had to say about Rick Briggs:

Rick Briggs, author of 'Knowledge Representation and Inference in Sanskrit: A Review of the First National Conference', is a senior engineer at Delfin Systems, 1349 Moffett Park Drive, Sunnyvale, California 94089. Briggs is currently working on natural language processing, numeric and symbolic coupling, and expert system development in the Artificial Intelligence Laboratory at Delfin Systems.[53]

Delfin Systems appears to have been a defence contractor to the US government. But it was certainly not part of NASA.

While hunting around for Rick Briggs in journals and archives, I stumbled upon an original Usenet posting for the 1986 conference in Bangalore.[54] It reads as follows:

Conference announcement:

First National Conference on Knowledge Representation
and Inference in Sanskrit
20-22 December, 1986
Bangalore, India

Sponsored by the Computer Society of India

For information write to:
Dr. T. M. Srinivasan
Madras Institute of Technology
Madras 600-036, India

or

Rick Briggs
Delfin Systems
2001 Gateway Pl, Suite 420
San Jose, CA 95110
408-295-1818

---

[53]Rick Briggs, 'The First National Conference on Knowledge Representation and Inference in Sanskrit', *AI Magazine*, 1987, p. 99.

[54]'Conference on Knowledge Representation and Inference in Sanskrit', *Soc.Culture.Indian*, 27 September 1986, from <https://groups.google.com/forum/#!original/soc.culture.indian/3nOflWkr1-8/WWoFFRVzG2gJ>, accessed on 14 March 2014.

Unless Briggs moved to Delfin Systems from NASA immediately after writing his original piece, it seems unlikely that he was a NASA scientist. Perhaps he was a contractor. But no more.

Yet, for over three decades, the myth of NASA's obsession with Sanskrit has grown and grown. Not only that, it has exploded into dozens of independent factlings that have gone on to have highly fruitful fraudulent lives of their own.

Since then, erroneous references to Briggs's paper, mostly by people who haven't read it, have found their way into news stories, books and other research papers. Many of them are embarrassing to read. Some feeble attempts have been made on some online communities to correct this error. But the efforts have had little impact. A Google search for 'Sanskrit Rick Briggs' currently yields around 51,000 results.

Still, the relative youth of this 'India fact' also makes it the easiest to explore and analyze. And the easiest one to set right.

But what happened to NLP research? Did those investigations into Sanskrit yield results?

Unfortunately, by the 1990s, NLP had moved into a new phase that was dominated by machine learning and statistical algorithms. Therefore, computers compare sentences against vast databases of information they have already processed, look at the similarities, context and probabilities, and guess at meanings. This is much the same way that most search engines work these days. When you punch in 'Low-fat Mutton Biryani Recipe' into Google, there isn't a piece of code somewhere breaking down that phrase into parts and then passing them through a rules framework. Instead it looks for appearances of this phrase in historical chunks of text, and tries to infer meaning from that context.

This new statistical approach, that depended more on large

archives and less on elaborate rules, made the grammato-logical approach less important, thereby, I suppose, somewhat moderating the need to study Sanskrit closely. At least from the perspective of its utility in artificial intelligence and natural language processing.

There is little to indicate that Rick Briggs's original paper was dubious in any way. Or that he was part of some larger conspiracy by a secret Pro-Sanskrit Illuminati. In fact, for all the frenzied chest-thumping India pride it continues to generate, the paper really did provoke a lot of research work in several Indian universities. In the course of research for this chapter, I kept finding references to Briggs's paper in much more recent work from Indian and foreign institutions.

By all accounts, Sanskrit seems to be a riveting language to study and understand. Not only does it have a fascinating grammatical framework, but it also has social and geographical aspects to its history that I think would make for interesting reading.

Unfortunately, like many other India facts, more energy seems to have been spent in parroting dubious glories and NASA certifications rather than in actually exploring the genuine merits of Sanskrit. In the course of polishing off this chapter and giving it a final coat of varnish, news emerged that the government of India had announced the appointment of a Second Sanskrit Commission.

The First Sanskrit Commission was organized in 1956. The Commission report said:

> The grievance of the people was acute because they had expected that there would be a better and more sympathetic understanding for Sanskrit after Independence. The appointment of the Sanskrit Commission may, therefore, be said to reflect the Union Government's keen awareness of this

feeling and their sincere desire to develop Sanskrit Education
and Research in the country on proper and fruitful lines.[55]

How dire was the state of Sanskrit then? The First Commission
sent out a survey questionnaire in English and Sanskrit to 'about
4,000 persons and institutions throughout India, who were
interested in or were concerned with Sanskrit Education and
Research'.[56] They received 1,200 replies, only 470 of which were
in Sanskrit.

On 23 December 2013, the Human Resources Development
Ministry announced, not a minute too late I suppose, the Second
Sanskrit Commission. And then, one week later, the original
circular was removed and all traces of it were deleted from the
ministry's website. What happened in the intervening week? *The
New Indian Express* speculated two theories:

> One version is that the HRD Ministry did not include a
> Sanskrit scholar from Panjab University in Chandigarh, the
> alma mater of Prime Minister Manmohan Singh, in the
> commission and that the circular was withdrawn after the
> ministry was pulled up for this 'error of judgment'.
>
> Another story doing the rounds is that HRD Minister
> Pallam Raju developed cold feet after taking the decision,
> as he was told that creation of a Sanskrit Commission in
> an election year would be dubbed as a move to appease the
> majority community.[57]

[55]'Report of the Sanskrit Commission 1956-57', from <http://www.
teindia.nic.in/mhrd/50yrsedu/u/45/3Z/453Z0101.htm>, accessed on 4
February 2014.

[56]'Report of the Sanskrit Commission 1956-1957', Ministry of
Education and Culture, Government of India, New Delhi.

[57]Cithara Paul and Anand Kumar, 'The Vanishing Act of Second
Sanskrit Commission', *The New Indian Express*, 13 January 2014.

Meanwhile, decades after the Briggs paper, computers are no closer to being programmed in Sanskrit.

SCEPTICAL PATRIOT INDIA FACT SCORECARD

Popular fact
Sanskrit is the best language for programming computers. (And all the other 'facts'.)

Score
3/10

Suggested fact
Sanskrit has a highly developed tradition and history of grammatical study that makes it better suited to some methods of machine translation and understanding than several other languages. Exploring the grammar and logic of Sanskrit may yet yield insights into the grammar and logic of artificial intelligence.

Homework for the excessively sceptical
1. What is the deal with NASA, man?
2. Why does Sanskrit have such a unique grammatological framework?
3. What is the state of Sanskrit research in Indian universities today?
4. Why not read Rick Briggs's original paper? It is freely available online.

SEVEN

The Doors of the Castle

In the summer of 2012, I spent a long weekend at a lodge thirty-five miles or so outside Edinburgh with the missus and her family. Our plan, as usual, was to sit around and do as little as possible, besides eat and drink, of course. The lodge, it turned out, also had a massive outdoor hot tub with views over the most spectacular rolling Scottish hills and copses and a little village far away in the distance that must have housed no more than a few hundred people. So we spent most of that weekend chlorinating away in the tub, or slumped in plump sofas, watching Andy Murray win Wimbledon on the TV.

But then, you can't possibly go all the way to the Scottish Borders district and not do at least a few jolly touristy things in Edinburgh. So the father-in-law and I spent a heady afternoon at the Scotch Whisky Experience (audio tours available in Hindi!), whilst the missus and her sister-in-law went around asking random Scottish men for directions just to hear that accent over and over again. And, of course, we visited Edinburgh's most important building, the splendid castle that sits on a hill overlooking the entire city.

Edinburgh Castle doesn't have the loftiness of some of Bavaria's finest royal residences, the air of reverence of Windsor Castle, or the symmetry and comprehensibility of Buckingham Palace. Indeed, it is a classic case of the whole doing no justice to the parts within. For, Edinburgh castle is actually very enjoyable indeed despite it being an asymmetric, lopsided heap of masonry. It is full of interesting little things from a dog cemetery to a little chapel that you can book for weddings, and I recommend a trip with your family without any reservations whatsoever.

In May 1573, Edinburgh Castle fell to a siege. Not because the attackers subdued the people inside. But because during the course of the siege, the castle began to slowly run out of water, until cannon bombardment destroyed a tower that fell into an important well. The thirsty defenders surrendered shortly thereafter.

I picked up a whole lot of other interesting castle facts on that trip. Often, castles have at least one, or even several narrow gateways through which visitors need to pass before reaching any of the main buildings. Often, these entrance pathways go steeply uphill. The idea, I was told, was to make sudden ingress as difficult as possible. And to make defence easier. What could be more convenient, and fulfilling, than pouring boiling pitch or burning oil on an invading horde backed up around narrow doorways as they struggle uphill on slippery cobbles?

But what if an invader actually fought his way in? Yet another obstacle was placed in his path in the form of narrow spiral staircases. These staircases were often built into the ground floors of the more important buildings that housed the king or the treasury. 'The staircases were too narrow to swing weapons inside,' a guide explained. 'The spiral design made it impossible to ride up them on a horse. And just a few defenders could hold back dozens of attackers.'

Later, when I went back home and returned to my research for this book, one thought kept coming back to me: India's natural geography makes it the perfect fortified castle.

This is by no means an original idea. I am pretty sure I've

read this analogy in the introductions to several books on the subcontinent. But the trip to Edinburgh, combined with some of the research for the chapter you are about to read, really hit that idea home.

The waters on three sides of the subcontinent form a formidable moat. For centuries, these seas isolated it from foreign influence and intrusion. On the remaining side, up in the north, the highest mountain range in the world forms an insurmountable barrier. Nothing, except the gods, can thrive in those icy heights. It is too high and too cold for any army.

But like every castle, India too had a narrow, perilous opening that intruders have tried to cross at their own peril. Wave after wave of emperors and barbarian hordes crashed into this narrow door up there in the northwest corner, just past the fertile, life-giving, civilization-feeding soils of the great rivers and their valleys. Some were brave and brutal enough to fight their way through. A few managed to establish footholds in this strange, exotic land. But only a handful saw these footholds grow into empires and dynasties; most found too many spiral staircases to negotiate on this side of the mountain passes and river valleys.

And for all these reasons—fertility, civilization, brutality— this northwest passage into India has the most intriguing history of any region in the subcontinent. Everyone who was anyone came this way. The Greeks, the Persians, the fearsome Central Asian tribes, the British, the Afghans...

Centuries later, it still remains a flashpoint. Cross the wrong line at the wrong place, and you're dead.

So it is of little wonder that some of the great Indian cities of old are to be found in this part of the subcontinent. All that cultural turbulence and enriched soil created great melting pots. From Mohenjo-daro and Harappa to Lahore and New Delhi, the northwest frontiers of India became the natural home of some of antiquity's most important urban entities.

Yet, the most interesting of all these cities, perhaps, is one that today lies in ruins. For a thousand years, it was one of the most important urban landscapes in all of India. Invader after invader crashed through the region. Yet, this city thrived. Not because of its fortifications or military might. But because of its intellectual worth, its ability to assimilate, and its shrewd capacity to negotiate rather than fight. It produced some of India's greatest thinkers, artists, scientists, theologists and princes. Some of the most illustrious kings in history enjoyed its hospitality.

It is also one of the great 'India facts' in itself: Takshashila.

❖

Persepolis, far away in modern-day Iran, was once the capital of the largest empire on the planet. Today, it is one of the world's great historical sites, some 550 miles from Tehran in Iran's Shiraz province. At the high point of their might, some people estimate, the Achaemenids who built Persepolis ruled over approximately half of the world's population. This they accomplished thanks to a combination of robust kingship, an excellent administrative system, a strong army and a civil service that was centuries ahead of most other places on earth. Their empire was huge, no doubt, but their social and cultural influence spanned across imperial boundaries of space and time. Alexander the Great adopted some of their court customs. The Athenians made some Achaemenid social customs their own.

They were also perhaps the first kings to leave their marks on the frontiers of their empire in the form of inscribed royal edicts—something other kings, especially Indian ones, started doing later. And more than one empire that came after them directly and indirectly adopted Persian methods of imperial command and control. Indeed, the modern word 'satrap', meaning a local ruler subservient to a greater power, was coined and popularized in Persia. A 'satrap' is what the Achaemenids called their local governors. (You could write entire world histories through the etymology of just this single word. Linkages from the original forms of the word satrap can be traced forward and across time to words such as 'shaher', meaning city in Arabic, Urdu and Hindi, and perhaps even the word 'kshetr'.)

Nothing encapsulates the enduring influence of Persia and the Achaemenids like the great ancient language, Aramaic. Draw up a list of people who spoke various forms of this language, and you have a power-packed historical who's who: Darius I, Jesus Christ and, quite possibly, Alexander the Great.

The extremely Eurocentric nature of Christian art and scripture might give you the impression that Jesus was a gorgeous chestnut blonde with milky-white skin who spoke in flawless Latin. But in reality, he was probably a sunburnt chap, roaming around a sunburnt land, speaking Aramaic, the lingua franca of the time. All thanks, in large part, to the Achaemenid decision around 500 BCE to make Aramaic the official administrative language of the empire.

Persepolis was the centre of the Achaemenid universe. And even in its current ruined form it is still glorious enough to make poets of historians, archaeologists and CIA spies. In 1969, historian and writer, Donald N. Wilber described the ruins of Persepolis like this:

> At sunset its stones glow with tints that change with the deepening dusk from yellow to pink to deep red and once again the ancient structures appear to be engulfed by the flames of long ago. Or on another occasion, under a cloudy,

wintry sky, the stones appear black, dark brown, and gray, a somber sight that evokes the lines of Omar Khayyam…[58]

Wilber seems like a charming chap, but he wrote these words just sixteen years after secretly helping to orchestrate the overthrow of Iran's Mohammed Mosaddegh government and reinstating the Shah.

In wondrous Persepolis, their great capital, the Achaemenids decided to flaunt the expanse and wealth of their empire in a unique way. On the walls of the great palaces and tombs at Persepolis, they not only inscribed lists of names of their conquests but also did something entirely different: They sculpted in figurative representations of the native peoples of these far-flung lands. Dozens upon dozens of these reliefs were cut into stone. In some places, they were shown as a procession of nations, bringing offerings to the Achaemenid king. In other places, rows of these subjects were shown holding up royal tombs. Each nationality was designed differently, with different clothes, weapons, hairstyles and head-dresses. Look closely, and you can even see earrings on some of them. It was a remarkably visual and permanent way of representing an empire's geographical reach—a photo album of conquest finished in stone.

There are Libyans here, and Arabs and Babylonians and Bactrians and Armenians and Parthians. Then, in one place, on the side of a massive staircase leading up to the ruins of the Apadana Palace, there is a group of three figures. Wilber writes:

Group 18 shows the Hindush (Indians). All but the leader are bare-chested and barefooted and wear the familiar dhoti.

---

[58] *Persepolis: The Archaeology of Parsa, Seat of the Persian Kings* (New York: Thomas Y. Crowell, 1969), p. 1.

They bring baskets containing vases, carry axes, and drive
along a donkey.[59]

These figures appear more than once across Persepolis. They
are all citizens of the twentieth satrapy, or province, of the
Achaemenids—the satrapy they called Hindush but more
modern writers call Sindh or, to be more specific, Takshashila.
Perched on the northwest corner of the Indian subcontinent,
by the banks of the Indus, this satrapy would later evolve into a
kingdom by itself, then a capital of a larger kingdom, and then
into an intellectual metropolis. There, weathering wave after
wave of invasions, and dynasty after dynasty of overlordship,
it lasted for a thousand years, before finally succumbing to the
unstoppable erosions of history.

Along with Pushkalavati and Purushapura (modern
Peshawar), Takshashila was one of the three main cities of this
region known as Gandhara. The Takshashila reliefs at Persepolis
are a fascinating reminder of the interconnectedness of India's
history and the tremendous geographic scope of ancient
empires. (The distance from Persepolis to the site of Takshashila
in modern Pakistan is almost exactly the distance from New
Delhi to Kanyakumari.)

But looking at the sculpture you'd be tempted to think that
the satrapy of India/ Hindush/ Sindh/ Taxila/ Takshashila was
just one of many small outposts of Achaemenid might. In fact,
it was one of the most important:

> The Satrapy of Taxila was the most heavily populated and
> richest of all the satrapies in the Achaemenid Empire.
> Herodotus mentions in *Histories* that this satrapy paid an
> annual tribute of 360 talents of gold dust…which was about

[59] *Ibid.*, p. 91.

one third of the tribute paid by all the 20 satrapies in the
Achaemenid Empire.[60]

Yet, it is not for wealth, grandeur, vases, donkeys or shotes that
Takashashila was renowned for in the ancient world. Instead, it
was a great pan-national centre of education in the subcontinent.
It drew scholars, princes and teachers from across the land, and
perhaps even from across the seas and mountains that fortify
Castle India. It taught the rich. It taught the poor. It finds
mention in ancient chronicles written in places as far apart as
Greece, Sri Lanka and China.

Therefore, it is understandable why Takshashila is the basis
for perhaps the most frequently repeated 'India fact': that
Takshashila was the first university in the history of the world.

⟪∴⟫

In the summer of 2005, a month or so after graduating from
business school, I joined a management consulting firm in
Mumbai. I would leave the firm in ten months or so, but I was
able to glean enough of the consulting business—consumers,
providers, rules of engagement, eccentricities—to later write a
series of comic novels about a management consultant's career.

Shortly after joining the company, I was told that the standard
procedure for new recruits was to attend a week-long orientation
programme that would give us the analytical, mathematical and
organizational tools needed to do our jobs well. Later, all geared
up to consult our asses off, we would sit and chat a few times
with somebody from Staffing. This functionary's job was to size
up our strengths, weaknesses and interests. She or he would then

[60]Rafi-us Samad, *The Grandeur of Gandhara* (New York: Algora Books,
2011), p. 34.

allocate us on projects all over the country or, if we were nice and productive, the world. Foreign posting! Yay!

In my case, none of those things happened, not even a token orientation over a cup of machine coffee with an admin underling. Maybe somebody somewhere didn't get a memo. But I spent a few weeks just sitting around in the office, helping out senior colleagues with spreadsheets and bar charts, before being sent to several auto component factories for a series of week-long due diligence projects. There was very little consulting involved.

Mostly these due diligence studies had me spending a week having a look around the factory, poking into account statements and inventory reports, and finally telling an investor if he should bother putting money into the company. After several months of this tiresome but not tiring routine, I was suddenly summoned into a room one day to meet an apparition from the Staffing team.

'Do you like higher education? Education policy? Government policy? That kind of thing?'

'Yes! I love education policy!'

I was only half-lying. I really did have strong thoughts about India's 'education problem' and did want to make a difference in any way at all. But a large part of me simply wanted to somehow get on to a real project.

'Great. We've got just the project for you...'

A billionaire non-resident Indian had realized that it was time for him to 'give back' to India. And he had decided that the best way to do this was to invest a billion dollars—to start with, much more to follow—in a new, world-class, multi-disciplinary university modelled along the lines of Stanford or Harvard. The billionaire had serious ambitions. He wanted to hire the world's best teachers to live and work in a modern world-class campus, purpose-built on thousands of acres of land. He wanted railway stations to bring students, air strips to fly in professors, cutting-edge architecture to house the classrooms and world-class laboratories to 'win India Nobel Prizes'.

It was, as you might imagine, the sexiest new project in the company. We spoke to great teachers all over the world, negotiated with numerous state governments in India to gauge interest in housing the institutions, and grappled with a national education policy that beggars belief. (For instance, it is substantially easier for an Indian citizen to donate large sums of money to a foreign university than to an Indian university. The tax and accounting rules are just mind-boggling.)

However, I soon realized some surprising things about universities. For instance, you don't actually get a very good university for a billion dollars. At most, you'd get a university with ten thousand students on the rolls, without any expensive laboratories, that mainly taught the humanities. Harvard, it is estimated, spends almost four billion dollars a year to cater to some twenty-two thousand students. I repeat, four billion dollars every single year.

No wonder then that a few months into the project we had to reassess all our assumptions. The billion dollars, a number we flaunted in meetings and presentations all over the country, wouldn't even make a ding in India's educational system. And it certainly wouldn't come close to winning India a Nobel Prize in the sciences anytime soon. (We once spoke to a researcher at a major university in Hong Kong who everyone agreed was poised to win the prize for Physics any day now: 'Oh, we're very close,' he said, 'just another ten or fifteen years of work.')

So, one by one, we began to shed our ambitions. Until all we were left with was a plan for a small, high-class institution that would deal with some science and a lot of humanities, and would hopefully draw in enough future funding from other donors, the government and the billionaire himself, to grow into a Harvard.

Over time, the consulting work reduced itself into two pieces: one was building a business plan for the university that estimated sources and uses of funds; the other was trying to convince state governments to donate land for the institution.

Which was when I was plucked off the project and asked to attend an orientation programme for new employees in Mumbai. This came six or seven months after I'd joined them, which was bizarre. The orientation programme itself was no less bizarre. One speaker left halfway through a lecture because he had to play golf. Another one didn't turn up at all. On the final day, I had a row with a senior partner about some HR policies that had both of us fuming. 'If you don't like how we do things, why don't you just quit?' he screamed. So I did. (But not before I had to go back to my business school campus for one last presentation as an employee. I told a classroom full of students why they should all join the company. This happened literally as the guys back in the office were drawing up my full-and-final pay cheque. It is, perhaps, the least honest thing I've done in my whole life.)

It was the politics of land acquisition in India that finally killed the project. After dragging on aimlessly for another six or seven years, it appears the project has now been shelved. No Nobel Prizes are forthcoming.

But there was one part of the whole 'University Project' that I found fascinating. And that was a history of Indian higher education my colleagues and I drew up as part of our research database (in the form of PowerPoint slides, of course). Irrespective of how we tackled this history, and whatever sources we used, it always had its roots in one of two concepts.

The first was India's great *guru-shishya* tradition, a tradition of wholesome mentorship that is referenced widely in our history, religion and epics. The popular visual representation of this cultural artefact is that of a bearded old man sitting under a tree, surrounded by a small group of devoted pupils devouring his every word. He taught them everything from the natural sciences to archery to the art of kingship. The *gurukula* was a residential school, with the students spending several years under the guru's tutelage. The guru was often rewarded with a token payment, if at all. The guru's real reward, I suppose, was the satisfaction of teaching itself. Though many seem to have been influential advisors to protégés who went on to become kings and emperors.

The second anchor concept was one of primacy. The fact that in the form of Takshashila, Nalanda, Kashi and other ancient cities, India was home to the oldest universities in the world. Time and time again, in the course of my research, references would pop up to Takshashila's antiquity.

Over and over again, one claim was made: Takshashila was the world's first university. We faithfully parroted and regurgitated this idea in all our presentations and interviews.

After all India did have the world's first university...

We have a great history of educational institutions. There was one up north and one even older than the one in Athens...

Why don't we start our presentation with a picture or a painting of Taxila and really drive home the point that...

But is Takshashila really the oldest university in the world?
It shouldn't be hard to find out, right?
Wrong.

✺

The primary problem here, once again, is one of definition. What really is a university? The temptation is to define the term with too much or too little specificity. Both cause problems for us.

If we define it too loosely—say, a large group of people learning a variety of subjects, all at the same place—then 'universities' could have started millennia ago. Who knows if small groups of students assembled outside the Stonehenge every morning? Perhaps they attended courses such as Advanced Stone Dragging, Large Circle Drawing, Travel and Tourism.

Defining it too closely also causes a problem. Limiting the idea of a university to modern notions of a central administrative authority watching over several schools with classrooms—and students who are filtered through a selection process—seems unfairly severe. It automatically rules out sophisticated schools of learning, with undisputed histories, that have existed all over the 'civilized' world. The University of Bologna, established in 1088, is widely noted as the earliest modern university. Yet, it is pre-dated by important schools in Athens, Nalanda and Baghdad.

So how do we start our sceptical journey of discovery?

I've decided, with not a shred of authority, to define a university as follows:

A geographical location, dedicated to the cause of learning, that imparts education in a range of subjects, year after year, for large numbers of students. Courses must be imparted by several teachers. And, most importantly, the centre should be important enough to draw students from a large geographical area. The larger the better. Drawing students from across various imperial and national borders would be most excellent.

Great.

So what do we know about Takshashila?

First of all, we know that it was situated within the Gandharan region, even though it seems to have often existed as a kingdom by itself on several occasions. We've already spotted the Hindush man at Persepolis. This chapter would have been 200 words short, or even shorter, if the Achaemenids had also sculpted in a man from Takshashila dressed in a 'University of Takshashila, since 1500 BCE' sweatshirt. Alas, this is not the case.

References to Takshashila abound in the great Indian epics. Both the Ramayana and the Mahabharata mention the city. The Ramayana mentions the city in some detail. Section 114 of the *Uttarakandam*, the last book of the Ramayana, tells the story of how Bharata, Lord Rama's brother, engaged in terrible battle with the armies of the 'Gandharva' province by the banks of the river Sindhu. After an initial stalemate, Bharata unleashed the arrow Sangharata, or 'fire of dissolution'.

Having bound them all with the noose of death and sundered them with Sangharata, Bharata despatched all the Gandharvas to the abode of death. Even the Devas could not recollect if such a dreadful encounter had happened before.

In a moment, the huge Gandharva army was slain. After the destruction of the Gandharvas, Kaikeyi's son Bharata set up two excellent and prosperous cities in the province of Gandharva. And he placed Taksha in Takshasila and Pushkala in Pushkalavati.

Both the cities were filled with profuse riches and jewels and covered with various gardens. As for many ornaments, it was as if both of them vied with one another. By just purchases and sales, and by the conduct of the people, the cities grew highly charming.

Both of them were filled with gardens and conveyances. Rows of shops were well arranged by the streets in both the cities. Both of them were adorned with many excellent fancy articles, picturesque houses, charming palaces and many beautiful and high Tila, Tamala, Tilaka and Vakula trees.

Having reared up those two cities within five years, Rama's younger brother, the mighty-armed Bharata, son of Kaikeyi, returned to Ayodhya...

It goes without saying that dating real places, or estimating their historicity, on the basis of mentions in the epics, is always prone to controversy. Indeed, there are those who believe that the entire *Uttarakandam* is a later addition to the Ramayana and not part of the original epic work. And thus has much lesser claims to accuracy or authenticity.

Thankfully for us, archaeological work carried out from the early twentieth century onwards helps us arrive at better dates for Takshashila's antiquity.

Much of the archaeological information we know today about Takshashila is owed to the leadership, vision, hard labour, literary efforts and good fortune of John Hubert Marshall.

Marshall makes a good case for being the most important archaeologist in India in the last hundred years. Born to a lawyer in West Dulwich, Marshall studied at King's College, Cambridge, where he won the 1898 Porson Prize for translating verse into Greek, a skill of wide-ranging utility. In 1902, at the age of twenty-six, Marshall was appointed the Director General of the Archaeological Survey of India by Lord Curzon, the Viceroy. Marshall seems to have taken over after a period of continuous turbulence that had left the ASI knee-deep in pending reports, delayed excavations and all round mayhem.

Marshall changed everything. He established standard operating procedures for archaeological work, revamped publishing schedules and, most importantly, began to include Indians in the ASI's work. He also prepared ground for what later became one of the most important finds of all: the Indus Valley Civilization sites at Mohenjo-daro and Harappa that were re-discovered in 1921. By then, Marshall had already completed almost a decade's worth of remarkable work at the Takshashila site. His first major book on the excavation, *A Guide To Taxila*, was published in 1918. He was still writing about the site in the 1950s. It was a pursuit that would consume him completely.

It is well worth reading Marshall's writings on Takshashila across his long career. It is fascinating to see how the established understanding of Takshashila's history keeps improving and evolving over this period. Marshall's 1918 first edition of *A Guide to Taxila* is a cautious work, wary of making too many assumptions and arriving at too many conclusions. His work of the 1950s, *Taxila: An Illustrated Account of Archaeological Excavations*, has the authority and confidence of a textbook. By then, it seems, Marshall was capable of speaking about the site, its history and its archaeology with much less ambiguity.

'There can be few archaeologists now living who have devoted as many years to the excavation of a single site as I have devoted to Taxila,' Marshall wrote in the preface of the later work. 'The manifold discoveries made in the course of those twenty-two years have thrown a flood of new light on the political and religious history of the North-West...'[61]

In the light of my own skin-deep explorations into the history of Taxila, this is a tremendous understatement.

Marshall suggested that there were not just one or two cities at the Taxila site but at least twelve, each older than the other. Yet, the oldest remains at the site, Marshall wrote, goes back no further than 600 BCE. Marshall even suggested, with great caution, that the establishment of the earliest cities at Takshashila may have been coterminous with the Achaemenid invasions.

---

[61] *Taxila: An Illustrated Account of Archaeological Excavations* (India: Bhartiya Publishing House, 1975), p. XV.

Did the Persians establish a new city at the Takshashila site as something of an imperial outpost? Or did they expand a smaller settlement that already existed at the time? We will never know. Thankfully, for the purposes of this investigation, we don't really need to know how it came about. As long as it did. An establishment date of 600 BCE for Takshashila already makes it 1,600 years older than the University of Bologna and Oxford, and some 200 years older than the great Platonic Academy in Athens.

But when did it become a centre of learning of regional, national and even international repute?

This is, of course, much harder to date.

Takshashila, Marshall wrote, is mentioned as a centre of learning in the Jataka Tales. The Jataka Tales is one of the central bodies of Buddhist literature. It tells the story of the various births of the Buddha. One English translation of the Jatakas prepared in 1907 indicates around fifty references to Takshashila across all the various tales.[62]

In the second section of the 'Thusa Jataka', one story starts like this:

> Once upon a time when Brahmadatta reigned in Benares, the Bodhisatta was a far-famed teacher at Takkasila and trained many young princes and sons of brahmins in the arts. Now the son of the king of Benares, when he was sixteen years old, came to him and after he had acquired the three Vedas and all the liberal arts and was perfect in them, he took leave of his master. The teacher regarding him by his gift of prognostication thought, 'There is danger coming to this man through his son. By my magic power I will deliver him from it.'[63]

[62]The Jataka, Vol. III, translated by H.T. Francis and R.A. Neil (London: Luzac & Company Ltd., 1897).

[63]*Ibid.*, Verse No. 338.

The 'Dummedha Jataka' starts another tale thus:

> Once upon a time when Brahmadatta was reigning in Benares, the Bodhisatta was reborn in the womb of the Queen Consort. When he was born, he was named Prince Brahmadatta on his name-day. By sixteen years of age he had been well educated at Takkasila, had learned the Three Vedas by heart, and was versed in the Eighteen Branches of Knowledge. And his father made him a Viceroy.[64]

Over and over again, the Jatakas tell us that princes were sent to Takshashila when they were sixteen years old; there they were taught the Vedas and eighteen branches of knowledge. Even if we take these tales with a massive pinch of salt, there is no disputing the fact that by the time the Jatakas were written, Takshashila was already being seen as an important centre of learning. Note that even the king of Benares, an important centre of scholarship in itself, sent his son to Takshashila. Surely this city was some kind of IIM Ahmedabad of the ancient world?

But when were the Jatakas written? The answer is not particularly helpful. Much of the Jatakas is commonly dated no earlier than around 500 CE, though this by no means rules out much older versions. And to make things even more complicated, there are no references to Takshashila in the oldest of Buddhist works, the *Sutta Pitaka*, dating back to around 30 CE.

If only there was a reference to educational activities at Takshashila that we could date more accurately...

There is. Kind of.

✳᭪✳

[64]The Jataka, Vol. I, translated by Robert Chalmers (UK: Cambridge University Press, 1895), Verse 50.

When Alexander the Great invaded his way into the northwest part of India around 320 BCE, he was accompanied by historians (a function now served by iPhones). Accounts by these historians mention Takshashila and a king called Ambhi. Ambhi, these histories say, seized the opportunity to enter into an alliance with the Greek juggernaut in order to protect himself and to settle longstanding rivalries with other local kings. Later Greek historians prepared their own compilations of these early histories. One account of Takshashila by the historian Strabo, written before 20 CE, is germane to our investigation:

> Aristobulus says that he saw two of the sophists at Taxila, both Brachmanes; and that the elder had had his head shaved but that the younger had long hair, and that both were followed by disciples; and that when not otherwise engaged they spent their time in the market-place, being honoured as counsellors and being authorized to take as a gift any merchandise they wished; and that anyone whom they accosted poured over them sesame oil, in such profusion that it flowed down over their eyes; and that since quantities of honey and sesame were put out for sale, they made cakes of it and subsisted free of charge; and that they came up to the table of Alexander, ate dinner standing, and taught him a lesson in endurance by retiring to a place nearby, where the elder fell to the ground on his back and endured the sun's rays and the rains (for it was now raining, since the spring of the year had begun); and that the younger stood on one leg holding aloft in both hands a log about three cubits in length, and when one leg tired he changed the support to the other and kept this up all day long; and that the younger showed a far greater self-mastery than the elder; for although the younger followed the king a short distance, he soon turned back again towards home, and when the king went after him, the man bade him to come himself if he wanted

anything of him; but that the elder accompanied the king to the end, and when he was with him changed his dress and mode of life; and that he said, when reproached by some, that he had completed the forty years of discipline which he had promised to observe; and that Alexander gave his children a present.[65]

Strabo also recounts another description of these 'sophists' or philosophers by one Nearchus:

Nearchus speaks of the sophists as follows: That the Brachmanes engage in affairs of state and attend the kings as counsellors; but that the other sophists investigate natural phenomena; and that Calanus is one of these; and that their wives join them in the study of philosophy; and that the modes of life of all are severe.[66]

Put together all these references from Buddhist and Greek literature...and it seems beyond all doubt that Takshashila was a great centre of learning. The city seems to have been rich with sophists—or teachers—with disciples. They were respected by society and seem to have been sustained at public cost. Remember that all these accounts come from the time of the Greek incursions, around 300 BCE.

Marshall then suggested that these centres of learning may have further flourished under Greek patronage. Surely there must have been some exchange between the Greek and Takshashila schools? It seems entirely likely.

Now the only two pieces of the puzzle left are those of definition and primacy. Takshashila was an education centre

[65] *The Geography of Strabo,* Vol. VII (USA: Loeb Classical Library Edition, 1932), p. 106.
[66] *Ibid.,* p. 116.

of great importance. But was it a university? And was it the first?

Takshashila ticks many of the boxes.

Researchers agree that the city had many teachers, perhaps divided into monastic school centres. These teachers taught a variety of subjects to students who travelled to Takshashila from all over the region. The Jatakas suggest that a few years here was a rite of passage for any young man of noble birth. Some writers have suggested that the students travelled here all the way from Korea.

Archaeological evidence has thrown up few remains of lecture halls or classrooms. But that can easily be explained by the fact that much of this education may have been imparted on a one-to-one basis. It may not have been a 'university' in the usual sense, but there is enough here to satisfy most people.

Finally, we come to the issue of its date of origin. Assuming that Takshashila was established in 600 BCE, as Marshall's archaeological work indicates, it seems probable that it developed into a university town by the time the Greeks arrived. Perched on the frontiers of this landmass, at the confluence of trade routes and battlefields, Takshashila must have been open to tremendous cultural flux. Marshall wrote:

> ...for we can hardly doubt that the interchange of eastern and western ideas during the period following the Persian conquest must have done much to stimulate the spread of knowledge, and that this stimulus became increasingly stronger under Maurya and Greek rule in the third and second centuries BCE.[67]

---

[67] *Taxila: An Illustrated Account of Archaeological Excavations* (India: Bhartiya Publishing House, 1975), p. 43.

The presence of 'sophists' in the region by the third century BCE can only mean that by then Takshashila had indeed become a centre, if a fledgling one, of learning.

I think we have enough evidence here to suggest that by around 300 BCE Takshashila had become something of an ancient university town. But does that make it the oldest?

Just about. Give or take a few decades.

The closest any other centre of learning anywhere else in the world comes to Takshashila in terms of antiquity is the Platonic Academy in Athens. This was founded around 387 BCE by Plato and flourished till approximately 600 CE. Which, incidentally, was about the time a final invasion by the Central Asian White Huns destroyed Takshashila once and for all. It was, I suppose, just one invasion too many.

Still, there is plenty here to make us proud. And plenty to make us think. But more on the thinking bit later.

SCEPTICAL PATRIOT INDIA FACT SCORECARD

Popular fact
Takshashila housed the oldest university in the world.

Score
7/10

Suggested fact
Takshashila housed one of the oldest major centres of learning in the world. It went on to seed a network of universities all over India, and coexisted along with a great Greek school of antiquity.

Homework for the excessively sceptical
1.   How feasible it for a city to go from being a little settlement in 600 BCE to a university town in 300 BCE?

2. How reliable are these Greek re-tellings of Alexandrian histories?

3. Do you disagree with my definition of what a university should be? How so? Does this change the conclusions we make in this chapter?

4. Why not plan a trip to Taxila?

5. A history of the Archaeological Survey of India might sound a bit 'meta'. But it seems tremendously exciting, does it not?

EIGHT

Quotes about India
A Reality Check

Along with numerous 'India facts', the other tool of the gullible patriot is a collection of India 'quotes'. Usually attributed to prominent Western thinkers, writers and scientists, these quotes are repeated *ad inifinitum* in everything, from bad newspaper articles to bestselling non-fiction titles. But are all these quotes authentic?

✳✳✳

India was the motherland of our race, and Sanskrit the mother of Europe's languages: she was the mother of our philosophy; mother, through the Arabs, of much of our mathematics; mother, through the Buddha, of the ideals embodied in Christianity; mother, through the village community, of self-government and democracy. Mother India is in many ways the mother of us all.

Popularly credited to: Will Durant, American historian.

Provenance: This quote is from the very beginning of Will Durant's 1930 book *The Case for India*.[68] Durant, a Pulitzer Prize

---

[68]Will Durant, *The Case for India* (New York: Simon and Schuster, 1930), p. 4.

winning writer, was a lifelong admirer of Indian philosophy and intellectual history. This book is a once-banned powerful expose of British atrocities in India.

✹✿✹

> India is the cradle of the human race, the birthplace of human speech, the mother of history, the grandmother of legend, and the great-grandmother of tradition. Our most valuable and most instructive materials in the history of man are treasured up in India only.

Popularly credited to: Mark Twain, American author and journalist.

Provenance: This is a somewhat shortened version of a longer line from Mark Twain's 1897 travelogue, *Following the Equator.*[69] The travelogue reveals a man fascinated by everything about India: the people, the buildings, the animals, the crime, the religion… And this fascination is not all positive as the quote above might lead you to believe. The full line in the book is as follows:

> This is indeed India! The land of dreams and romance, of fabulous wealth and fabulous poverty, of splendor and rags, of palaces and hovels, of famine and pestilence, of genii and giants and Aladdin lamps, of tigers and elephants, the cobra and the jungle, the country of a hundred nations and a hundred tongues, of a thousand religions and two million gods, cradle of the human race, birthplace of human speech, mother of history, grandmother of legend, great-grandmother of tradition, whose yesterdays bear date with

[69]Mark Twain, *Following the Equator*, Vol. II (New York: Harper and Brothers, 1809), p. 26.

the mouldering antiquities of the rest of the nations—the one sole country under the sun that is endowed with an imperishable interest for alien prince and alien peasant, for lettered and ignorant, wise and fool, rich and poor, bond and free, the one land that all men desire to see, and having seen once, by even a glimpse, would not give that glimpse for the shows of all the rest of the globe combined.

Perhaps it is understandable why the excised quote is used more often. The book is a spectacular read.

꙰

We owe a lot to the Indians, who taught us how to count, without which no worthwhile scientific discovery could have been made.

Popularly credited to: Albert Einstein, you know the guy.

Provenance: There seems to be no primary reference to this quote in any book or in collection of Einstein's papers. It also does not appear in Princeton University's *The Ultimate Quotable Einstein*, a work that otherwise has several India references. This is not to say it is not true. But Einstein holds the dubious distinction of being credited with other people's quotes.

꙰

If I were asked under what sky the human mind has most fully developed some of its choicest gifts, has most deeply pondered on the greatest problems of life, and has found solutions, I should point to India.

Popularly credited to: Friedrich Max Mueller, German Indologist.

Provenance: In 1883, Max Mueller published a collection of lectures he had previously delivered to candidates for the Indian Civil Service at the University of Cambridge. This quote is from the first of those lectures, titled 'What India Can Teach Us'.[70] It is a remarkably powerful piece of prose that exhorts students to look into India's past—not present—to seek a more meaningful life. Mueller offers up India to these students as a land ripe for learning and experimentation.

> You will find yourselves everywhere in India between an immense past and an immense future, with opportunities such as the old world could but seldom, if ever, offer you. Take any of the burning questions of the day—popular education, higher education, parliamentary representation, codification of laws, finance, emigration, poor law—and whether you have anything to teach and to try, or anything to observe and to learn, India will supply you with a laboratory such as exists nowhere else. That very Sanskrit, the study of which may at first seem so tedious to you and so useless, if only you will carry it on, as you may carry it on here at Cambridge better than anywhere else, will open before you large layers of literature, as yet almost unknown and unexplored, and allow you an insight into strata of thought deeper than any you have known before, and rich in lessons that appeal to the deepest sympathies of the human heart.

Powerful stuff. And relevant today as it was all those years ago.

✻✿✻

[70]Max Mueller, *India: What Can it Teach Us?* (USA: Book Tree, 1998), p. 31.

India conquered and dominated China culturally for twenty centuries without ever having to send a single soldier across her border.

Popularly attributed to: Hu Shih, former Ambassador of China to the US.

Provenance: Hu Shih was a renowned Chinese diplomat, writer and liberal. He also seems to have had a slightly less 'China-centric' view of Chinese history that may have isolated him from his peers, especially in a period when the Communist nation was flexing its muscles. Part of this view was the idea that Indian religion had heavily influenced ancient China. In a lecture at the University of Chicago, Hu Shih once talked about the advent of a great 'cultural invasion' from India around the first century BCE:[71]

> The Chinese people were dazzled, baffled, and carried away by this marvelous religion of rich imagery, beautiful and captivating 'ritualism', and wonderfully ingenious metaphysics. There was not only a heaven, but thousands of heavens; not only a hell, but eighteen hells of ever increasing severity and horror. The religious imagination of the Indian people seemed so inexhaustible and always of such marvelous architectonic structure. China readily acknowledged her crushing defeat.

Yet, all my research has not managed to pin down that original quote to any Hu Shih work or lecture. Many early online instances of the quote attribute it to a piece by Hu Shih in a

[71]Hu Shih, 'The Haskell Lectures, University of Chicago', 1933, from <http://csua.berkeley.edu/~mrl/HuShih/ReligionChinese.html>, accessed on 15 March 2014.

1999 issue of *Bhavan's Journal*, a magazine published by the Bharatiya Vidya Bhavan educational society headquartered in Mumbai. But Shih was long dead by that date, having passed away in 1962. It also appears that this particular issue of the journal may have published several other 'India quotes' that similarly have gone on to become popular.

The probability remains that the original quote is from a Chinese language source that is no longer widely available.

✳✦✦✳

I have travelled across the length and breadth of India and I have not seen one person who is a beggar, who is a thief. Such wealth I have seen in this country, such high moral values, people of such calibre, that I do not think we would ever conquer this country, unless we break the very backbone of this nation, which is her spiritual and cultural heritage, and, therefore, I propose that we replace her old and ancient education system, her culture, for if the Indians think that all that is foreign and English is good and greater than their own, they will lose their self-esteem, their native self-culture and they will become what we want them, a truly dominated nation.

Popularly attributed to: Thomas Babington Macaulay, member of the Supreme Council of India between 1834 and 1838.

Provenance: The best must always be kept for the last. If there is any investigation of provenance in this book that can eventually lead to house-burning, this is it. Thankfully, several other people have debunked this particular quote before me. So, if you must burn houses in outrage, start with theirs please.

Macaulay may have only spent four years in India. But he did have plenty to say about the colony, its peoples and its complex network of values, morals, ethics and intellectual perspectives. A lot of it was not complimentary. He is most widely remembered, and vilified, in India for his 'Minute on Indian Education' delivered to the Parliament in London on 2 February 1985. Macaulay's observations on the past and the future of Indian education later culminated in the English Education Act of 1835, a set of reforms that gave weightage to education in English over that in the native languages. Angst about this continues to simmer in India to this day.

However, this quote appears nowhere in any of Macaulay's works. It is certainly not a part of Macaulay's famous 'Minute'. Nor does it appear in any of the copies of his collected works that I have been able to access.

Believers in the quote point to it as a clear sign of Macaulay's devious plans in imposing English on Indians. Detractors of the quote—there are a brave few—dismiss it because it is too appreciative of India. And Macaulay, they often say, hated everything about India.

The truth, of course, is much less extreme. Macaulay was not a blind Hindu hater. In 1840, he wrote an essay on Robert Clive for *The Edinburgh Review*, in which he wondered why the English know so little about India:

> We have always thought it strange that, while the history of the Spanish empire in America is familiarly known to all the nations of Europe, the great actions of our countrymen in the East should, even among ourselves, excite little interest. Every schoolboy knows who imprisoned Montezuma, and who strangled Atahualpa. But we doubt whether one in ten, even among English gentlemen of highly cultivated minds, can tell who won the battle of Buxar, who perpetrated the

massacre of Patna, whether Surajah Dowlah ruled in Oude
or in Travancore, or whether Holkar was a Hindoo or a
Mussulman. Yet the victories of Cortez were gained over
savages who had no letters; who were ignorant of the use
of metals; who had not broken in a single animal to labour;
who wielded no better weapons than those which could be
made out of sticks, flints, and fish-bones; who regarded a
horse-soldier as a monster, half man and half beast; who took
an arquebusier for a sorcerer, able to scatter the thunder and
lightning of the skies.

The people of India, when we subdued them, were ten
times as numerous as the Americans whom the Spaniards
vanquished, and were, at the same time, quite as highly
civilized as the victorious Spaniards. They had reared cities
larger and fairer than Saragossa or Toledo, and buildings
more beautiful and costly than the Cathedral of Seville.
They could show bankers richer than the richest firms of
Barcelona or Cadiz, viceroys whose splendour far surpassed
that of Ferdinand the Catholic, myriads of cavalry and long
trains of artillery which would have astonished the Great
Captain. It might have been expected that every Englishman
who takes any interest in any part of history would be curious
to know how a handful of his countrymen, separated from
their home by an immense ocean, subjugated, in the course
of a few years, one of the greatest empires in the world. Yet,
unless we greatly err, this subject is, to most readers, not
only insipid, but positively distasteful.[72]

This was written well after the famous 'Minute'. And it is by
no means the words of a man who detests all things Indian.

That original quote, however, seems to be either a fabrication
or a misattribution. The definitive debunking of this quote was

[72]Thomas Babington Macaulay, *Critical and Historical Essays Contributed
to the Edinburgh Review*, Vol. 3, London, 1870, p. 1.

published by the Belgian writer, Koenraad Elst on his website.[73] Elst suggests that the quote was the outcome of some dubious paraphrasing, first published in *The Awakening Ray*, the journal of the Gnostic Centre in New Delhi:

> The 'quotation' is introduced with the qualifier: 'His words were to this effect.' So there you have it: Macaulay never said this. The alleged quotation came into being as a mere paraphrase...

Still, this hasn't prevented the quote from being used over and over again in everything from books and (gasp!) blog posts to presidential addresses and even reports by government departments.

❈❦❈

In closing, I would like to present my favourite Internet 'India factsheet' of all time. I tend to receive a link to this compendium of three facts—it always appears as a set of three—at least once a year. It is truly ludicrous.

Even if nothing else in this book amuses you, I am really hoping this will.

> Please forward this email to as many Indians! Right now, India is the richest country in the world! Wonder how? It's really amazing.
>
> (1) It's due to Mr G. Vaidyaraj, who donated all his wealth, about which he actually did not know. He is a descendent of Raja Krishnadev Raya from Mysore district. For the last three hundred years or so, three

[73]'A Dubious Quotation, A Controversial Reputation: The Merits of Lord Macaulay', from <http://koenraadelst.bharatvani.org/articles/hinduism/macaulay.html>, accessed on 16 March 2014.

stones were worshipped in his house. But nobody tried to see what these were, except this person, who is a lawyer by profession. One day, when there was nobody in his house, he took one of the stones out to see what it was that they worshipped. Due to the dust deposited on it, from many, many years, it looked only like a simple stone. But when he touched it, some portion of the stone was cleansed. And he saw a bright ray of light. He saw something which attracted his attention. And he was amazed when he cleaned all of them. The whole room was filled with light. He discovered they were diamonds of about 4,600 carats each. He informed the Government of India and the news is censored... The stones are deposited in a Swiss Bank. The cost of a single diamond exceeds the GDP of USA+UK. Even the World Bank does not have enough money to buy it. India can buy virtually seven developing nations. One diamond costs thrice the debt of the World Bank over India. One such diamond can buy ten Bill Gates for you. And the World Bank has proposed to the Indian government that it can pay India in installments... India's GDP is 34.25 billion dollars. Bill Gates's property is ninety-five billion dollars approximately, so that is the way 'nature changes'. Our Prime Minister has refused to sell it. He said it will be sold or mortgaged for credit when we need it. Otherwise, right now, we have no problems. You can go through *The Times of India*, [which had] a small column on it a week ago. Star TV presented a 115 minute documentary on it about fifteen days ago. *The Hindu* [carried a] half page article in it. After that it was censored as classified.

(2)   Another [piece of] good news is that in the Desert of Thar, a deposit of oil and natural gas has been found. This stores what Kuwait has in its stomach. India can

go with this ONGC energy reserve for another 30 years. And moreover, it can export it to other counties. It's incredible! But true.

(3) An Indian boy in his twelfth standard has disproved Einstein's 'Theory of Relativity'. Shocked? Read on... Sudarshan Reddy has theoretically proven the existence of a sub-atomic particle, which can travel at speeds greater than that of light, thereby challenging one of the fundamental postulates of the 'Theory of Relativity'. In his recent research paper submitted to the Institute of Advanced Physics (IAP) at Trieste (Italy), Sudarshan has proved the existence of a class of sub-atomic particles called leptons, which can travel faster than light. The international physics community is shocked by this discovery. Dr Massimo Martelli, President of the IAP, has this to say about the paper submitted by Sudarshan. 'After long, careful and critical analysis, I can confidently say that Sudarshan's research papers show a tremendous leap in our understanding of physics. His investigation [analyzes] "leptons". His work builds substantially on the work of Einstein and others in the field of relativity.' When physicists from Princeton University tried to measure Sudarshan's IQ with an IQ-metre (at the American Embassy in Delhi), the meter broke down. Sudarshan, incidentally, is the brother of Madhu Reddy, the Indian whiz-kid who developed an operating system superior to Microsoft Windows. We should all be very proud of these boys.

Please forward this email to Indians!

Please don't.

NINE

Why History and Scepticism Matter

Many years ago, when I was no more than fifteen-years-old, I went with my family on a trip to Kochi, one of Kerala's, and India's, great cities.

Cough.

Okay, fine. Maybe Kochi isn't a melting pot of cultures like Mumbai, a cesspit of corruption like Delhi, or full of Bengali women like Kolkata. The one thing going for Kochi, however, is tremendous historicity. Kochi's colonial experience is diverse, complicated and deceptive.

I say deceptive because Kochi isn't full of the large buildings, monuments and landmarks that you would have come to associate with a city that has such historical and commercial provenance. The one exception to this rule is the giant crane emblazoned with the words 'Cochin Shipyard', which stands watch over the city's port district like a massive orange cubist elephant. Otherwise, all you see are unassuming, unexciting buildings that take some effort to be appreciated. But once you do put in the hard work, everything pops with detail and life. There are stories all over Kochi. (But no Taj Mahals.)

One such somewhat underwhelming Kochi landmark is the Dutch Palace in Mattancherry. Back when I first harangued my family to take me there, it was mostly a collection of empty rooms curated very poorly. (Since then the palace has had a superb makeover, with excellent signs and a well-explained, world-class permanent display.)

I tried to make the most of the visit, reading every signboard, poring over every mural. The rest of my family just pointed and laughed at everything.

'Hey, guys! This is a mural of the old king taking a dump!' Roars of laughter. 'Look, Sidin,' someone would say, pointing at a piece of sculpture, 'this is the most historic sculpture in all of Kochi... Oooooohhhhhh...' Guffaws.

To this day, more than fifteen years later, I still feel hurt and frustrated.

'Don't laugh at this,' I had burst out, half in tears, at one point. 'Maybe you don't understand. But don't laugh at these historical things...'

Of course, many of these very same people look at shots of London or Paris or Rome on TV and lament: 'Those Europeans are not like us! They respect their history...'

Yet, every time I besieged the non-fiction section in a bookstore, or cracked open a book on the Second World War, or switched to a documentary on TV, I got the same questions: 'What is the point of reading all this? How does it matter? What can one possibly achieve by trying to understand the lives of all these dead people?'

A few years ago, I wrote a blog post about how Indian school textbooks dealt with post-Independence history very unevenly. Most textbooks, at least the ones I was issued, liked to go on and on about the Non-Aligned Movement, the victorious wars with Pakistan, and even about how much India participated in the United Nation's peacekeeping programmes.

References to the Kashmir issue, the loss to China, the Emergency, the anti-Sikh riots... they were all glossed over in the vaguest possible terms—if they were referred to at all.

While writing this book, I repeated the exercise I performed when I wrote that original blog post. I downloaded the latest copies of history and social science textbooks released by the National Council of Educational Research and Training (NCERT).

Right away, I must admit that the textbooks have vastly improved since my days in school. They are no longer endless chunks of text broken by the odd picture. Instead, they seem to aspire to greater interactivity, original thinking and analysis, and less committing to memory. (Though I wonder how well this new approach is being used in schools.)

And, yet, the textbooks seem to cover an even shorter span of post-Independence history than they used to. The latest edition of the NCERT's history textbook for Class XII has an introductory section called 'Defining the Focus of Study'. This section, which outlines the NCERT's approach to history education, starts as follows:

> What defines the focus of this book? What does it seek to do? How is it linked to what has been studied in earlier classes? In Classes VI to VIII we looked at Indian history from early beginnings to modern times, with a focus on one chronological period in each year. Then in the books for Classes IX and X, the frame of reference changed. We looked at a shorter period of time, focusing specifically on a close study of the contemporary world. We moved beyond territorial boundaries, beyond the limits of nation states, to see how different people in different places have played their part in the making of the modern world. The history of India became connected to a wider inter-linked history. Subsequently in Class XI we studied Themes in World History, expanding our chronological focus, looking at the vast span of years from the beginning of human life

to the present, but selecting only a set of themes for serious exploration. This year we will study Themes in Indian History. The book begins with Harappa and ends with the framing of the Indian Constitution.[74]

Thus the final textbook that many Indian schoolchildren will study in their last year of school ends with the Indian Constitution, and makes no attempt to touch upon the last six decades of Indian history. Before coming to any conclusions, I went back to the Class VIII textbooks to see how far they went.

That textbook explains events up to the first two five-year plans of Independent India, followed by a section on the Non-Aligned Movement, and then abruptly ends with a section titled 'The Nation, Sixty Years On'. The section ends on a sobering yet somewhat uplifting note:

> The Constitution recognizes equality before the law, but in real life some Indians are more equal than others. Judged by the standards it set itself at Independence, the Republic of India has not been a great success. But it has not been a failure either.[75]

Then an odd section on the Sri Lankan civil war is bolted on. And then the book ends.

If my survey of these books is accurate, this means that each year India produces thousands upon thousands of eighteen-year olds who have little to no instructed idea of the last sixty years of Indian history. They have no idea if or how those five-year plans worked. They have no idea if or how the Non-Aligned Movement worked. They have no idea about the numerous wars India has fought against Pakistan or China. They have no

[74] *Themes in Indian History: Part I* (New Delhi: NCERT, 2008), p. vii.
[75] *Our Past III: Part II* (New Delhi: NCERT, 2008), p. 171.

idea, for instance, of what many people call the greatest threat to India's internal security: the Naxal movement. What created this Naxal movement? And why is the movement popular where it is? Our youth doesn't know.

When I wrote my original blog post in 2005, several people wrote back to me saying that there was no need for children to know all this. 'Why should they know we lost a war to China? If we tell them, they will grow up without pride in our army and country.' Some even said that children were too young to understand the nuances of the Kashmir issue. Instead, they said, we should let them arrive at their own conclusions about recent Indian history.

Sometime in 2002 or 2003, a group of Japanese Hibakusha, or atomic bomb survivors, visited Chennai. The city was a stop on what I think was a global tour to promote peace and condemn nuclear weapons. In Chennai, they decided to visit a primary school and tell the students why the idea of nuclear weapons was a bad one. Since the adults seem beyond proselytization, why not try with the brains of babes?

I read about the school visit in one of the local newspapers. I don't recall which one, and no amount of searching online has thrown up the original news report. But the broad details of what happened are seared into my mind.

After their presentation, the Hibakusha asked the children: Should countries go to war? No, they all said in chorus. Should countries use nuclear weapons? No! Should India use nuclear weapons? *Never!* What if the enemy is Pakistan? Oh, Pakistan is a special case, the kids said, we should totally nuke them.

Every time I retell this story at a public forum, there is an explosion of laughter...followed by an awkward silence.

These were primary school students—children too young to be taught any serious history in school, children much too young to appreciate any aspect of India's complicated relationship with Pakistan. And yet, these children had no hesitation in picking out Pakistan for a nuclear attack. Pakistan, to these tiny, partly formed minds, was already a special case—the great enemy.

Somehow, we've managed to create a social, cultural and political environment in which even our youngest citizens have been so deeply indoctrinated to hate. Who else, I wonder, have we indoctrinated them against? Little Muslim kids against Hindus? Little Hindu kids against Muslims? Little Dalits against all Yadavs?

Still, the people who manage our school curricula feel no need to actually teach them any aspect of post-Independence Indian history. This, despite the fact that the last six decades of Indian history have so much to tell us about the tensions that currently determine our political and social existence.

Why should each generation be brought up on the selective prejudices of the one before it?

I believe that this is exactly the point of history. And not just reading or studying history but also approaching it with a sceptical bent of mind. When each generation approaches received wisdom with scepticism, perhaps it will reassess established notions of right and wrong, love and hate. Perhaps it will finally see mistaken priorities for what they really are.

Perhaps it will do something that previous generations steadfastly refused to do.

✻✿✻

As I am writing this book, India is gradually gearing up for a new round of general elections. So far, there is little real debate over policy or reforms. But there is plenty of vague posturing and pointless name-calling.

Recently, one senior BJP politician said that the spread of the English language had hurt India's culture. There is little to indicate that he said this after any rumination or with a larger point to make. But supporters and critics immediately felt the need to take sides on the 'English' issue.

A few weeks before that, there was yet another controversy when the Congress announced that it would pass a Food Security Bill into law through an ordinance instead of waiting to debate it through Parliament (perhaps hoping to use it as a populist vote-gathering scheme). Instantly, there was widespread debate over the benefits and pitfalls of such a bill.

Then there was the tragic case of the mid-day meal poisoning in Bihar. On 16 July 2013, children died after a consuming a mid-day meal at a government school in Chappra, Bihar. At the time of writing, it appears that the oil used to cook the meals was contaminated with insecticide. Instantly, a debate erupted about the benefits of a mid-day meal scheme, and if it was merely a vehicle of massive corruption.

Then there were two controversies of a more subjective nature. Was M.K. Gandhi a Hindu nationalist? And were the next elections going to be a face-off between the economic positions of Jagdish Bhagwathi and Amartya Sen?

I am not suggesting that history or scepticism by themselves can provide all the answers to all these questions. History, after all, is not a forward-looking discipline. It can only tell us what happened the last time, not what will happen next time. Similarly, scepticism is hardly sufficient to do anything but ask questions. But together they—history and scepticism—form a potent force for enquiry.

What is a food security bill? A sceptic would start from the basis—the document itself. Why this bill? What motivated it? How has India dealt with the problem of hunger before? How have other countries? What happened there? What happened here? What are the issues people have raised? Will it really increase inflation? Is higher inflation a problem? Will it increase labour prices? Is higher labour price a problem? Will it give the poor an incentive to be idle? What does the history of food programmes tell us?

All this might seem like an awful lot of questions to ask and history to read, to understand just one topic. Yet, all you need to accomplish this investigation is a computer and an Internet connection. And, most importantly, a mind that is either free of bias, or aware of its own bias and prepared to be proven wrong.

Imagine, then, if many more Indians began to investigate problems like this. Imagine if we learnt to rise beyond our received 'wisdom', email-delivered 'truths' and feel-good 'history'.

Then, one day, when a general or a bureaucrat or a minister, originally from Chennai, has to press the button that obliterates a city in Pakistan, he may stop for a bit, think and ask himself: 'Why?'

TEN

The Sceptical Patriot
What Is the Point of All This?

For the first twelve months of the writing of this book, there was actually very little writing. Coming to think of it, I don't think I wrote anything at all for at least the first nine months after signing the contract.

I spent most of that time researching the various chapters, creating lists of various 'India facts', and figuring out how frequently each of them appeared in blog posts, newspaper articles, Facebook updates and general conversation.

But, to be perfectly frank, I also spent a lot of time in a state of turmoil. What was the point of all this? Was I simply puncturing the glorious worldview a lot of people had about their own country? Sure, the pursuit for truth would be a reward in itself. But would this puncturing be worth it? What was constructive about telling a lot of people that their country was not really the richest country in the world once upon a time, or that their ancient language isn't really the uber-computer-programming language it is made out to be?

Throughout this period, whenever I spoke about the book, my wife kept asking me: 'Are you writing this to prove that a lot of Indian people are idiots? Or is there a greater point?'

This was a phase of the writing process I'd never gone through previously.

When you're writing fiction, your motive, at its basest, is merely to tell a good story. Perhaps you want to evoke certain emotions in the reader. In the case of my first three books, I wanted readers to laugh a lot and think a little.

When you're writing articles for a newspaper, you are, in one way or the other, trying to explain an issue of contemporary relevance. The exact topical connection, or 'news peg', may not always be direct or immediate. But there is always a rationale, a thematic or topical justification.

When I started writing this book, I struggled to find any of these motives. Sure, I wanted to entertain people—in some vague, page-turning way. I also wanted to convey some of my sense of general curiosity to the broader public.

But was there a higher purpose? A greater social, cultural or national virtue that I was trying to propagate?

Thank god for editors and publishers, and their ability to whip you about the face with a contract. Just as I was beginning to waver in my commitment, the editor who commissioned this book asked me to get a move on. Start writing, she said, and it will all fall into place.

And you know what? I think it has, at least from my writing perspective. (But given that you've read so far, I assume it has made some sort of sense from a reading perspective too.)

I know more about India today than I ever did two years ago. Much of this knowledge is of a highly specialized nature, such as the history of the Gandharan region or the various methods of natural language programming.

But as I thumped out chapter after chapter in a library or a hotel room or a cafe, a broader picture began to take shape.

And, I daresay, a deeper understanding of what actually makes India great.

This epiphany, or collection of epiphanies, is of an objective nature. Indeed, many of you may have read so far without remotely having felt any of those epiphanies. But, for me, they were unmissable. I'd like to talk about just three of my most important epiphanies

***

EPIPHANY NO. 1

There is really no such thing, ethnically speaking, as an Indian. Apart from, perhaps, the tribal people who live in some of India's densest jungles and faraway islands, there is no one in this nation whose genetic provenance is not the outcome of centuries of intermingling. An Indian who calls himself 'pure' is an Indian living in lala-land. We are all, every single one of us, the outcomes of centuries of civilizational upheaval. We are part-Greek, part-Mongol, part-Persian, part-British, part-Mughal, part-French, Part-Portuguese, part-Arab, part-Turk, part-everything.

Indeed, it would be entirely possible and plausible to draw up an individual's family line which starts from the cities of Mohenjo-daro or Harappa, winds its way through an Aramaic-speaking scribe in Taxila, through to a Buddhist satrap in the Gangetic basin, and thence on to a Hindu priest in the Deccan plateau, then a Muslim trader on the Malabar coast, before winding its way into an Anglo-Franco-Indian family in Pondicherry.

This is not imagination gone wild but history meandering onwards.

No doubt, there are many people here who feel that all this is a load of liberal, the-world-is-one-big-family nonsense. That this is the kind of hippie-nonsense that makes nations weak and citizens unpatriotic. Perhaps. But only when you reduce the idea of identity, patriotism and humanity to its crudest line-in-the-sand form.

Indeed, a true Indian, an Indian cognizant of the frenzied history of his or her past, must be proud not of his or her identity but of the utter lack of identity.

We carry in our blood not pure Hindu, Muslim or Christian platelets. On the contrary, an entire planet's worth of history courses through our veins.

And the average Indian does not need the expensive equipment or complex education of a genetic scientist to appreciate this lack of identity. He or she just needs to look into his or her lunchbox.

Right now, as I sit here on my couch, writing these words, I can look across my living room and see a small plastic box full of frozen *aloo gobi* thawing away on the kitchen counter. Earlier this week, my mother-in-law, who has been visiting us for a couple of months, decided to stack my freezer with food before she left. She flew back to Delhi just last night, and we've decided to 'miss' her by eating some of her world-famous *aloo gobi*.

There are potatoes and cauliflower in the dish, of course, but also green chillies, tomatoes, onions and an array of spices, powders and seeds.

The *aloo gobi* is perhaps to North India what apple pie is to America. It is cheap and easy to make. Like most Indian dishes, you can make *aloo gobi* in as complex or rudimentary a fashion as you wish. You can eat it with rice, rotis, parathas or even with sliced white bread. A little leftover *aloo gobi* between two slices of white bread, toasted in one of those clamp sandwich-makers, and served with ketchup and mint chutney, is one of the greatest breakfast achievements of our species.

Yet, just six hundred years ago, the *aloo gobi* was unheard of in India, not because it was some sort of state secret, but because potatoes, tomatoes and green chillies simply didn't exist.

The potato, tomato and green chilli are all vegetables that originated in South America and were brought to Europe by Spanish conquerors as part of what is now known as the 'Columbian Exchange'—a process by which South Americans gave the world a number of culinary treasures, and in return got enslaved and murdered.

The great food historian, K.T. Achaya estimates that tomatoes only got adopted by Indian cooking sometime in the 1880s, or even later. Potatoes were being grown in India around the time of Akbar's reign, but even a century-and-a-half later, British records tell us, they were seen as culinary novelties.

And yet, today the potato is one of the foundation columns of Indian cuisine. Can you even imagine a *pav bhaji*, a *dum aloo Kashmiri*, a proper Kerala mutton stew or a *masala dosa* without the potato? (No, you can't.)

Think about that for a second. In less than one century, an entire country, with about eighteen per cent of the world's population and impossibly diverse culinary cultures and preferences, went from looking at the tomato with suspicion to consuming it with absolutely everything.

Now, there are two ways of looking at this.

You can lament the ease with which we allow our 'culture' to be diluted. You can reject the foreign and glorify the native. You can lionize our 'Indian' history—whatever that means— draw a line across a period in time and reject everything that came afterwards.

When do we stop? Do we reject everything after the 1800s, and label everything before that as 'pure' Indian? Or do we draw the line at the first Mughal invasions? Or the first Greeks?

When does that line between 'pure' and 'corrupt' Indian begin to make sense?

Your guess is as good as mine.

Or you can celebrate our ability to absorb. From Greek invaders to Persian architecture to South American tomatoes—we absorbed everything. We integrated them deeply into our culture and identity and history.

Of course, none of this happened without turmoil and turbulence. No doubt, somewhere in India, there were pro- or anti-tomato riots that consumed entire societies. But today, those differences would seem ludicrous to us.

It all goes back to a question of identity.

What are we? What does it mean to be Indian?

Tough question. Perhaps this is why our ancient thinkers and philosophers always spoke of the self in such…amorphous terms. How can you be one thing when you are everything?

Aham brahmasmi. I am spirit. I am the cosmos. I am everything.

I can't even presume to understand the depth in that idea. But to me it means a sense of self that is all-encompassing, without boundaries. It reflects an openness to ideas—and a fluidity of identity.

And I think it is this approach to identity that has made this exasperatingly complex nation what it is today.

✦

EPIPHANY NO. 2

This is going to piss off a lot of people, and I am buying asbestos underwear as I type, but...we need to stop asking the history of centuries past to vindicate our actions today. History is not a manifesto for action, a list of crimes to be avenged, a litany of positions to be reversed or a collection of rights to be wronged.

History is, to paraphrase the great A.J.P. Taylor, the answer you give a child when he or she asks you: 'What happened?' It is a description of what happened. History, of course, can be biased in many, many ways. Every historical event can be told from multiple perspectives. Each perspective can yield diverse analytical and emotional responses. Each point of view can paint the protagonists in drastically different colours, occupying very different moral positions.

My own personal biases should easily be perceptible in this book. For instance, I give much greater weightage to records written in the period of history that I am studying than I do to any later analyses, however respected or canonical. This poses problems when studying periods of Indian history that are better documented in British records than Indian ones. Not to mention my linguistic bias—the vast majority of my sources are in English, and some in translation.

To me, this means that there are two very good reasons why you don't want to sit now, and try to cite historic reasons for your actions.

The first reason is simply one of causation.

How do you decide which wrongs to right?

Many people I know—Hindus, Christians and Sikhs—point to the Mughal invasion of India as a watershed moment that plunged India into chaos. Many believe that we are still living through the aftermath of this 'Muslim influx'.

There is no disputing that the Mughal invasion of India fundamentally changed the country. Native places of worship were razed, non-Muslims were massacred, populations were displaced, treasures were plundered and an 'alien' overlord was placed on the throne of India.

Perhaps you are one of those Hindus who feel a burning desire to seek revenge.

But then, what happens when the Buddhists of Sri Lanka decide that they are owed a pound of flesh for the Indian armies that invaded their country over and over again for centuries? Sri Lankan chronicles tell stories of Indian armies raping and pillaging their way through Buddhist towns and villages.

Or what happens when those who believe they are descendants of the Western Chalukya Empire decide they want revenge for the Cholan invaders who—but of course—raped and pillaged them?

Or do we only focus on atrocities committed by one religion against another? Or do we collectively decide to reset our history of atrocity and invasion at a random date, and begin seeking retribution for everything that happens after that?

Instead of any of this, why don't we just come to terms with our history?

No, really. Why not just say: 'You know what? Maybe I should be seeking justice for the future rather than seek justice for the past...'?

Just an idea.

Or we can keep killing each other.

The other reason why it makes no sense to right past wrongs is one of culpability. How can you possibly punish someone today for an atrocity you think one of their ancestors *may* have committed hundreds of years ago according to the one version of history you've read?

Sure, history may have been unfair to your religion, region or persuasion. Sure, there may be people out there today who inherited the fruits of the unfairness your ancestors were subjected to. But do you really want to live in a society that is scouring its past for open vendettas, and thereby creating new ones?

Or do you want to live in a society that looks ahead?

By all means, demand law and order in your lifetime. By all means, demand justice for crimes committed now. By all means, don't be one of those people who say: 'We should move on, *yaar!*' when you see injustice around you.

But draw the line somewhere.

One good idea is this: 'If they didn't do it, don't punish them.'

The Sikh who shot Indira? Take that bastard down! Random Sikh walking down the road? Not so much.

❋⚬❋

EPIPHANY NO. 3

This occurred to me around two-thirds of the way into the writing of this little book.

As I began investigating some of the genuine high points in Indian history—Takshashila, Ayurveda, mathematics, the Chola navy—I began noticing something about contemporaneous Indian society that facilitated these developments.

Now this analysis of mine is quite approximate. And trained historians will perhaps qualify these observations heavily. But I still think that there are some observations here worth thinking about.

All these high points in Indian history occurred in societies that were open, turbulent but peaceful, well-administered and curious.

They were open societies in the sense that these innovations often took place in cities or towns that saw tremendous human movement. Takshashila, for instance, was perched at something of a subcontinental crossroad. A hundred cultures washed in off its intellectual shores. Besides, it was a university town that ostensibly had students come and go from all over.

These were turbulent yet peaceful societies, in the sense that even when kings and emperors came and went, they managed to keep their institutions of learning and teaching intact and flourishing. They recorded their knowledge in the forms of books that were translated and transported widely.

Many of them were well-administered societies. They thrived especially well when they were governed by stable, sophisticated governments that invested in infrastructure and the tools of administration. The Chola navy, for instance, is widely believed to have been a public-private partnership between the king and the Cholan merchant guilds.

But most of all, these innovations came from a society that seemed to celebrate curiosity and a spirit of enquiry. The Jataka Tales tell us that students at Takshashila were often taught for free. Poor students were funded by the government. Teachers taught a variety of subjects. Students often spent years learning this variety of subjects. Takshashila and the other university towns of Nalanda and Kashi, we are told, even taught students from penniless families. And all this happened, much like in the golden age of Arab science and mathematics, not divorced from faith but energized by it.

There are many lessons for modern India here.

For instance, perhaps we need more cities that foster more intermingling of people with various talents and skills to create more innovation.

Perhaps, we need more state support of institutions that

foster enquiry, criticism and scepticism. Rather than scale up an educational system that is so focused on vocational training and employment, we need to create a Takshashila-like environment, where the only qualification for a student is a sense of inquisitiveness and a willingness to work. Perhaps, like the princes of the Jataka Tales, all administrators could use a short, sharp dose of general education before they get to work.

Perhaps, we need a system of government that provides continuity without being stagnant or risk-averse, a system of government that respects institutions.

But most of all, we need a society that refuses to conform, that refuses to put up social, political and ideological borders. Perhaps, we need to go back to being the great cultural sponge that we once used to be.

Maybe then, we will stop harking back to our glory days and a long list of dubious 'India facts', and create a few new ones.

Acknowledgements

First of all, I would thank my missus. I have no idea how she copes. Somebody should write a book about this. She would very much like it if you bought this book in large numbers so that she can quit and open a bakery.

Next, I would like to thank Pradipta Sarkar who called me up one day and asked me if I would like to write a non-fiction book about anything. Sheer madness. If it weren't for that call, this book would have remained a gleam in my eye.

I would like to thank Kapish Mehra, Ritu Vajpeyi-Mohan, Dharini Bhaskar and everyone else at Rupa Publications. Thank you for your endless patience and your gullibility when it comes to my excuses for delays.

Sukumar Ranganathan, Priya Ramani, Siddharth Singh, Seema Chowdhry, Pradip Saha and everyone else at *Mint*: I am sending my story in fifteen minutes. Sorry.

Much of the preliminary research for this book was carried out with the help of my dear friend Jesal D. Sheth, her curiosity and her JSTOR account. Thank you Jesal *yaar*.

This book would have been completely impossible without the collections and the helpful staff at the British Library and the London Library. Libraries are some of the greatest achievements of our species.

I would like to thank Alex von Tunzelmann for persuading me to join the London Library. This book is immensely better for that piece of advice.

And finally, thank you Internet! You are so good. You are full of errors. But aren't we all?